MUSIC: HEALING
THE RIFT

MUSIC: HEALING THE RIFT

IVAN HEWETT

continuum
NEW YORK · LONDON

CONTINUUM

The Tower Building, 11 York Road, London SE1 7NX

15 East 26th Street, New York, NY 10010

www.continuumbooks.com

First published 2003

British Library Cataloguing-in-Publication Data
A catalogue record for this book is available from the British Library.

ISBN 0–8264–5939–0 (hardback)

Typeset by Aarontype Limited, Easton, Bristol
Printed and bound by MPG Books Ltd, Bodmin, Cornwall

꧁✿꧂

Contents

Acknowledgements

Thanks to Simon Holt, for hours of companionable listening; to Tony Sellors, for being a good sounding-board, and for his library; to my editor Mark Bolland, for putting this book back on course when it was threatening to go off the rails; and, most of all, Amanda for putting up with writer's grumps.

Foreword

Classical music is at a turning point. The ways in which the audience receives music are changing radically: the potential of the internet, causing turmoil in the record industry, and challenges to concert life mean that our traditional musical institutions are having to come to terms – rather too late, in many cases – with radical changes in audience taste and behaviour. These changes are not particular to music, and have affected all areas of our cultural life, but they are especially marked in the world of classical music because this is a world in which the past too often dominates: dominates the repertory, dominates modes of concert performance, and too often dominates the age of the audience. Previous generations of audiences up to the 19th century listened to (and performed more often than we do) essentially the contemporary music of their time: why that has changed, and why new music for an important period became uncommunicative is a major issue for us now.

FOREWORD

This vivid and stimulating book by Ivan Hewett is a thought-provoking essay on what has happened to music up to the end of the 20th century, and helps us to address the issues that confront it in the 21st century. As he writes, 'multiplicity is our natural state'. It could hardly be otherwise in a world which broadcasting and recording has transformed our experience of music. All manner of music, in all kinds of performances old and new, is available to us at the flick of a switch, on the train or in the shower: this creates a major challenge to the notion of musical tradition. Brahms wrote with Beethoven looking over his shoulder, acutely aware of his place in music's single line of development. Now, as Ivan Hewett vividly demonstrates, the major influences on composers and cultural life can come from anywhere, any time, any idiom. Multiplicity can be a richness, but it can also be disorientating.

Classical music still flourishes, and will continue to flourish as long as audiences value the excitement of live performance and listen to adventurous and innovative music alongside the tried and tested classics of the repertory. Each year at the BBC Proms we attract large audiences, new audiences and young audiences because the economic basis of the season allows to programme experimentally, always including new and rare works alongside the great classics. That bold balance is becoming rarer as orchestras and other institutions under financial pressure find it difficult to take risks: it may well be the smaller, flexible organizations that find it possible to best meet the needs of tomorrow's audiences.

Ivan Hewett brings the same individual, quirky questioning to this book that he brought to his years presenting BBC Radio 3's *Music Matters*, and which now informs his music criticism in the *Daily Telegraph* and elsewhere. I cannot think of a better and more stimulating guide to the myriad issues that confront the world of music today. Both serious and funny, unsensationalized and intelligent, this book may not offer all the answers, but it asks all the right questions and discusses them with penetration and insight.

Nicholas Kenyon
Director, BBC Proms

Introduction

Music is a strangely paradoxical thing. It is part of the human world, and yet somehow not part of it; when people are touched by it they are both reconciled to themselves (you could even say: revealed to themselves) and yet they're also lifted outside and beyond their own littleness. It is the most insubstantial thing in human life, mere vibrations on the air; but viewed another way it is mundanely real, the basis of a colossal global industry, the thing that anchors people to the present moment and to each other. It asserts boundaries, of nation and groups and cultures, it demarcates social spaces and co-ordinates and unifies great collective moments – funerals, declarations of war, political rallies. But it also spills over them. Music subverts our categories; it stirs up passions, rouses long-dormant memories. It can change its meaning, spill over its own categories of genre and style, leap across cultural boundaries, mingle itself with the very thing that, a moment ago, it asserted its difference from.

MUSIC: HEALING THE RIFT

This much has always been true of music. But in the early twenty-first century there are new reasons why music is hard to grasp. Part of the difficulty of engaging with music today is its bewildering ubiquity, variety and quantity. We are assailed by music of every kind, at every moment, with background music from elevators and restaurants, TV idents, advertising, and other people's Walkmans supplying an unwanted sound-track to our lives. And, amazingly, we pass between these fleeting musical experiences with only minimal discomfort. If we stand back and view the different types of musical experience available in the West, it's hard to find a connecting thread, some substratum of sound or action or meaning that we could find in common between them all. Along a single street in New York or London one might find Koranic chanting, a mother singing a lullaby, a string quartet rehearsal, a movie sound-track and hip-hop issuing from car windows. Where is the 'essence' here, the thing that allows us to say that these are all examples of that peculiar thing called music?

Of course there is no essence that any empirical investigation could discover. It follows that any book which addresses itself, in the manner of sociology, to the facts of musical practice as they exist on that putative street, will take that variety of incommensurable practices as its primary fact. But there is another way of looking at music, one which acknowledges that it is a value-laden discourse in its essence. To talk of the nature of music is like talking of human nature; it is an aspirational, or normative, category rather than an empirical one. That comparison is not inapt, because as George Steiner says, 'Our capacities to compose and respond to musical form and sense directly implicate the mystery of the human condition. To ask 'what is music?' may well be one way of asking 'what is man'?[1]

Every musical utterance, of whatever kind, is a bid for transcendence, so the idea of music made or received in a spirit of indifference ought to be inconceivable (though modern life, alas, provides plenty of examples of it). That transcendent aspect cannot be content with being simply good of its kind. The rap artist, the jazz pianist, the orchestral violinist all think of themselves as *musicians*, who use their particular skills and inherited musical culture to bid for something beyond themselves. As the guitarist Robert Fripp says, 'The musicness of music is eternal, the forms of musical organisation evolve within a culture.'[2]

There are plenty of books around which show that music can indeed be viewed with the indifferent, value-free gaze of the sociologist. But though these books give us all kinds of insights on the *use* of music, music in and of itself seems to pass them by (naturally enough, since for the authors of these books music is nothing more than the sum of its social functions). This isn't a view I can share. To stand even a chance of being illuminating about music itself, any book must share the normative aspiration of the subject-matter. The question then arises; which set of norms? Over the millennia, different conceptions of this ideal realm have emerged, some extra dimension of musical meaning beyond its function of lulling babies to sleep or uniting the guests at a wedding or funeral. That extra dimension may be religious, as in Koranic chanting; it may be imbued with a mystical cosmology, as in Pythagoras. Or it may have to do with a range of formal values and practices and meanings, definable only within the musical discourse itself, which one calls 'the musical'.

It is that third way of defining the musical realm, the one elaborated within Western classical music, that provides the focus for this book. To take classical music as the paradigm musical experience may seem an odd, even provocative stance in these culturally diverse times. But there are good reasons for doing so, because it is only within classical music that we find a fully articulated conception of the musical realm. Look closely at religious conceptions of the musical, and they soon dissolve into an aspect of dogma or theology; look closely at Pythagoras, or his numerous contemporary offshoots, and the conception of music elaborated there turns out not be musical at all. It is a kind of 'mystical mathematics of heaven', so close, in medieval times, to astronomy and geometry as to be virtually indistinguishable from them. And if we look at rival claims to the musical realm within contemporary practices, they are all to a degree parasitic on the classical realm. Writers on pop music, having first expatiated on the 'cultural signifiers' found so abundantly in pop music, can rarely resist the temptation to lapse into formal modes of analysis, showing that Radiohead's songs are good partly because they have exactly the kind of interesting asymmetrical ostinati one finds in Stravinsky. As for world music, the very fact that the category only has any meaning in the West (Ali Farka Toure is not a world musician to his fans back home) shows that its way of hearing and appreciating will be Western through and through.

However, there is an irony in choosing classical music as one's touchstone of musicality, because now is the moment when the very idea of classical music seems to be dissolving away at the edges. There is an identifiable core, made up partly of a historical repertoire – Bach to Shostakovich, plus a few pockets before and after – and those composers who still work in purely acoustic media like orchestras. But these days the creativity, and the focus of journalists' attention, is focused on composers working in new technologies, and on the border territories between categories. Where pop and classical meet, there is that strange territory called 'avant-rock' or 'un-pop', found in curious out-of-the-way venues like the Kitchen and on classical radio stations in the wee small hours. On the border of jazz and experimental music there is another interesting territory, peopled by improvisers like Evan Parker and composer/performers like John Zorn. Classical electronic music and 'electronica' seem to be moving ever closer. And on the borderland between world music and classical music there is a fertile territory opening up. Most fertile of all is a category that mixes all these areas, blending aspects of jazz, world music, electronica and classical music into a blend that promises to be rich, even if it doesn't always deliver.

But even in these areas, one finds the same old aspirations to that elusive thing called music. And again, when people want to judge these musics they reach, willy-nilly, for the old categories. They look for a balance of form and content (pieces shouldn't outstay their welcome, even those that set out to bore us), they look for a wide range of material balanced against formal cogency (that old chestnut 'unity in variety'), they look for the signs of a striking, original 'personal voice'. All these things were born when the idea and practice of classical music came into being; by which I mean, born as a self-consciously pursued ideal (which isn't to say one can't find formal balance, originality, well-turned melodies and so forth in every musical culture). It may be doubted, though, whether these new forms of music actually yield up their meaning when addressed with these categories. It may well be that they require new forms of evaluation altogether; in which case we may be driven to saying they have no real connection with classical music at all. Perhaps it's only institutional inertia, and the lack of a tailor-made space, that brings 'avant-rock' within the ambit of a classical music venue or radio station.

That is one question this book aims to address. But even before it reaches that point, it will have to deal with the ambiguities and tensions within the very idea of classical music. There's a tension between classical music as a historical phenom-enon, rooted in social and economic factors, and as a timeless realm, which to a degree floats free of history. (The two things of course go together. The reason classical music had such power at a certain historical moment was precisely because it cultivated a self-image of 'timeless permanence'.) Classical music becomes modern music when that reciprocity between inner and outer is broken. This allows the internal side of music – its ideas, its forms, its vocabulary – to run riot, uncon-strained by the need to serve any social need, or even to attract an audience. This is why modern music has been so exuberantly inventive of new sounds, new systems of composition, but rather poverty-stricken when it comes to imagining new social forms for music. Just keeping up with the technical changes in classical music is a difficult enough job, which is why most primers on modern music focus on the internal side of music, giving us at best an 'aesthetics of making'.

But of course there is the other side, the 'aesthetics of reception'. This is bound to be problematic, partly because of the mismatch between the new-fangled technical means of new music and its social apparatus, which until recently has clung to a nineteenth-century form. The time-lag is reflected in the categories people bring to new music, which tend to be the very same as those they bring to Tchaikovsky and Cole Porter. When these prove unfruitful, listeners cast around for help – and who better to help them than the composer? Thus we have that unfortunate reliance on terms of listening set by the composers themselves (when composers testily insist that audiences judge their music 'on its own terms' what they really mean is: judge it on *my* terms). This has given new music an unhealthily hermetic character, with a small coterie of composers, devotees and apologists all mutually confirming each other's specialized discourse. I've tried to break out of that circle. My aim has been to strike a balance between the how of new music and the why, sometimes allowing a technical innovation to suggest a new sort of musical meaning, at other times drawing on some current mode of evaluation not determined by new music discourse – 'authenticity', say, or 'evocation' – as a means of approach to an unfamiliar musical object. The other pitfall of books of this sort is that in the attempt to be comprehensive, they end up being little more than a list with a few summary descriptions attached. I've tried to keep the names to a minimum, focusing on a few individuals and pieces that seem especially significant.

The book is divided into nine chapters which trace a thematic rather than chronological narrative, though I've tried to preserve at least the outline of a historical thrust as well. The big theme is the crisis that overtook the laboriously constructed musical realm in the early twentieth century. It was a crisis that could be tackled in two ways. Some composers, the traditionally minded ones, have chosen to shore up that realm, often in a spirit of melancholy that recalls T. S. Eliot's line: 'these fragments have I shored against my ruin'. Others felt, and continued to feel, that the only way to preserve the integrity of that realm is to rebuild it entirely. It's an attempt fraught with irony, because this rebuilding is in fact no less restorative than the other, apparently more traditional way. At bottom, Boulez and Lachenmann, no less than John Adams, want to be seen as part of that great enterprise that includes Bach and Beethoven. Leaving aside the real radicals like

John Cage, there is always an aspiration – an aspiration all the deeper for never being spoken aloud – to reconstitute the musical realm so that it becomes whole again.

That crisis is described in Chapter 3, 'Things Fall Apart', which tries to show that the falling apart was as much occasioned by pressure from without the system as pressure from within. In Chapter 4, 'Multiplicities', the paradoxical situation this engenders, of a number of competing claims to the musical realm, is described. In Chapters 5 and 6 I bring the focus forward in time to the postwar period, to describe new attempts to refigure the musical realm from the inside ('Text, Body, Machines') and from the outside, as manifestations of a particular expressive value ('Authenticities'). Chapter 7 brings the focus closer still, to the last quarter-century or so, where the attempts to refigure the old musical realm (both its material and its meanings) are described ('Expression Makes a Comeback'). Chapter 8 moves on to describe the one form of musical aesthetic which seems to be the most symptomatic of the present moment ('The New Naivety'). Finally, in 'Rediscovering Music', I take stock of the incredible multiplicity of the art music realm, asking whether the category any longer has a definable meaning, and, if not, where the old aspiration to 'the musical realm' can now be realized – if at all.

But before that, some scene-setting. Chapters 1 and 2, like Chapters 5 and 6, are two views of a single subject, one from the angle of musical 'making', the other from the angle of 'receiving'. The subject is the creation of an autonomous musical realm, beginning in the sixteenth century and continuing until the late nineteenth. Chapter 2 looks at this extraordinary phenomenon from the outside, from the point of view of the values and meanings listeners and musicians invested in it. Chapter 1 takes the inside view, looking at the actual musical 'stuff' it was made from, and how this 'stuff' arose from a social revolution in the way music was used.

NOTES

1. Steiner, G. (1989). *Real Presences*. London, Faber & Faber, p. 6.
2. Green, L. (2001). *How Popular Musicians Learn*. London, Ashgate, preface.

1

❦

Depths and Shallows

'There are only two sorts of music; good and bad.' An oft-repeated and very useful principle, if we only knew what 'good' and 'bad' meant. At one time all music was good, in the sense that it was always the authentic expression of the social situation that called it forth. Alongside 'fitness for purpose' – and inseparable from it – was another criterion of 'good' music. The only music that was good was *my* music, meaning not music to my taste – as that phrase means today – but 'the music of my people'. Music, until recent times, was everywhere and always an assertion of belonging. To say that the two sorts of music – 'mine' and 'not-mine' – map exactly onto 'good' and 'bad' isn't quite right. Better to say that the two sorts divide music into 'music' and 'unutter-able screeching' – to borrow the phrase used by Des Voeux, British Governor of Hong Kong to describe Cantonese opera.[1] That phrase proves that the visceral, instinctive rejection of other cultures' music as not really being music at all is hardly confined to distant times and 'primitives' who haven't yet learnt to embrace cultural relativism.

But there is another reason to cherish music, a reason that has nothing to do with its 'fitness for purpose', or its power to assert a sense of belonging. It is a value that can be found in the most surprising places. When the Ghanaian musicologist Kofi Agawu returned to his home village he found singers shaped their songs with exactly the same scrupulous attention to formal balance, unity within variety, etc. that a Western composer brings to a symphony (a contentious finding, especially for those theory-minded musicologists who like their Africans to be comfortingly Other).[2] It has to be said, though, that these qualities only reveal themselves to the eye of the outsider (which to a great extent Agawu now is, having studied and taught Western music at American universities for the past 20 years). For the singer they are swallowed up in function; a beautiful lullaby is one that sends babies to sleep. Agawu's peculiar, distanced love for his own people's music is a late, ironic flowering of an idea born centuries ago in the West, that music could be prised away from its social function and contemplated for its own sake.

It takes an effort of imagination now to perceive just how egregious a moment this was in the history of music. Music, until then, had always been made to fulfil *this* particular role, in *this* particular place, with *these* musical forces immediately to hand. After a long life together, stretching over millennia, the Siamese twins of social function and music were falling apart. Of course the break wasn't momentary; it was a long process, which is by no means complete yet, and probably never will be. Music still accompanies weddings, state visits and raves, and when people listen to music in a concert hall the occasion is as much to do with asserting membership of a social caste as it is with savouring 'autonomous musical values'. Nonetheless, sometime in the modern era, the explosive idea that music was transportable took root.

When exactly is a moot point, though it must surely be bound up with the availability of leisure time – because only during leisure time can music be prised away from social function. In the late Renaissance, church music was enjoyed in lute transcriptions in aristocratic homes, and the bass patterns of dances like the *romanesca* turn up, newly embellished, in keyboard pieces. This shows how the notion of formal adaptability – arrangement, variation, embellishment – is an essential corollary of the notion that music is transportable. You can't take a mass movement as composed for a church choir and take it bodily into a new environment. It has to be rethought for a new, intimate medium. But this implies that the music is no longer identical with its first incarnation – there is something as it were 'behind' the Josquin mass movement, and its keyboard arrangement, which is common to them both.

This points to something of absolutely crucial importance, which is that when music becomes socially mobile, it changes its nature. What you might call music's internal side – its melodies, its interesting harmonic motions – springs suddenly into sharp relief. Paradoxically, it is the act of adapting music for a new space that calls attention to its peculiar individuality – something that, in the aristocratic home or church where it was born, is veiled by its function. But the act of inquiring into this individuality, so as to reshape it for new circumstances, itself requires a certain effort of abstraction. If five vocal parts are to be reconceived for the six strings of a lute, this raises the revolutionary idea that two pieces, so different at their surface, are at some level the same. This shows how a new social function actually created a new formal aspect of music – its ability to retain a formal identity under numerous transformations.

In aristocratic circles, the idea of 'listening to music' may have been well established by the sixteenth century, and the habit would soon spread downwards, to the emerging middle classes. In 1678 the 'small-coal merchant' Thomas Betterton

advertised one of the first public concert series in
Europe, given in a 'bung-hole' above his ware-
house in London. For that audience, gathered
together to hear music by Handel, Pepusch, and
Italian Baroque composers, the ready-made criterion of value – which you could describe coolly
as 'fitness for purpose' – was no longer available.
A new one was coming into being called taste, one
of whose elements – 'fitness for the occasion' –
was not so different to the one it was replacing.
Our enjoyment of Mozart these days is not much
concerned with Mozart's sense of the seemly
(indeed in Peter Shaffer's play *Amadeus* this side
of Mozart is played down, as it scarcely fits with
the idea of the wild, untutored genius) but for
Haydn it was vital – when he wished to praise the
young Mozart to his father, he was keen to say 'he
has taste'.

But taste is an elusive quality, and not just for us
who are embarrassed by the term. In the eighteenth century it was hard to figure out just what
kinds of music were 'seemly' and appropriate in a
music room. The answer 'those that give pleasure'
seemed dangerously circular. Eighteenth-century
thinkers fretted over whether music really was
one of the fine arts, and therefore deserving of
serious attention, or whether it was only an 'idle
tinkling', as Lord Chesterfield described it to his
son.[3] It didn't appear to imitate anything, which
seemed to rule it out. But one thing it could do was

stir deep emotions, and in the Age of Sentiment this made music highly prized. From being the most despised of the arts, music was suddenly elevated to being the most revered. Music's supremacy became a critical cliché, down through Walter Pater and Conrad (who called music 'the art of arts'). 'Taste', though, was fading, and in time Mozart's conviction that music must always be beautiful, even when expressing ugly emotions, was replaced by the notion that music had just as much right to deal in the ugly and the demonic as any other art.

Music was now caught up in the new critical discourse of sincerity, where the ugly could be sublime, and where prettiness was regarded with suspicion. Art was not meant to be pleasing, it was meant to be truthful, and in pursuit of that art would have to trample over rules of propriety. This had begun to happen long before Romanticism sanctioned these trangressions. Bach's music was condemned for its bad taste, in the sense that he mixed up the genres; he was apt to load his dances, which should be light and pleasing, with dense chromaticism and contrapuntal complication. The Romantics, though, aimed at something far more bold; they wanted to create an art entirely without conventions. Berlioz's *Romeo and Juliet* is neither an opera, nor an oratorio, nor a symphony, but some unprecedented mingling of all these. Schumann's character pieces have no forebears, they create an entirely new genre, but one without formal rules. Alongside the rejection of specific genres was a suspicion of anything that smacked of 'the middle ground'. Pieces were now outlandishly short (as in those Schumann character pieces, one of which – 'Sphinxes' in *Carnaval* – has no duration at all) – or outlandishly long. Wagner's *Ring of the Nibelungen* stretches over four evenings. Chamber music was now a problematic medium; the age expressed itself more naturally through the heroic exploits of a single virtuoso, or the stupendous effects of the ever-expanding Romantic orchestra.

Taste, which had once been a prerequisite for discerning truth (only a tasteful person could distinguish good music from bad) was no longer needed, because all art could communicate directly, without mediation. It could go straight 'from the heart to the heart' as Beethoven expressed it on the dedicatory page of his *Missa Solemnis*. Beethoven trusted that his Mass would reach everybody – we all have 'hearts', and anything written in music's universal tongue is bound to reach any heart. But this raises a dilemma. Like any music, classical music must appeal to a certain constituency – but how does one appeal to the universal constituency? Someone must be excluded, or else the category is a vacuous one. The solution was a difficult one, strenuous in its very essence. It was 'everybody' when perceived, or approached, at their best moments. Classical music appeals to our better natures.

What were the features of this peculiar kind of music? What gave it its claim to be simultaneously superior – and therefore by definition apprehensible only by the few – and at the same time universal? To put the question in that way is slightly misleading, in that there was no brand-new repertoire of 'classical music' called up to fit the new need and the new description. To begin with, classical music was simply the music people had always enjoyed – or, rather a portion of it – but redescribed, with certain features of the music now highlighted for particular attention. Historically, therefore, 'classical music', when it emerged, was tied to the rest of music – social music, folk music – by a thousand threads. But once those features had been highlighted, the repertoire of classical music became self-referential – new pieces were added to the body by self-consciously imitating those qualities. Once that happened, the threads that bound classical music to other music began to break – with lamentable results, as we'll see.

It wasn't only composers who enlarged the territory of 'classical' music. As the conception, and the institution of classical music took root, the 'way of hearing' that it engendered spread out to encompass other musics. Suddenly virtues could be seen in historically distant music that intervening ages had condemned as barbarous. Charles Burney, the English music historian of the eighteenth century, could not see any virtues in Renaissance counterpoint, which he condemned as 'Gothic', at that time a term of abuse.[4] It was only in the late nineteenth century, when the historicizing tendency in 'classical' music had gathered strength, that musicians could discover the same musical values in a sixteenth-century Palestrina Mass that they'd already discerned in a Bach fugue or Beethoven sonata. From there it was a short step to performing that Mass in the concert hall, an idea that, even as recently as Beethoven's time, would have seemed absurd.

Along with the process of expansion, both forwards and backwards in time, went a sharpening of exclusivity. The terms of admittance to the realm of classical music became more stringent, and less and less bound to the likes of the present moment. So, for example, Liszt's piano music was never admitted to the canon in the nineteenth century, with the exception of the B minor sonata (and still isn't today) whereas Chopin's works were published in a handsomely edited collected edition within a few years of his death. But while Liszt's works were rejected, Couperin's were being welcomed in – Brahms, who more than anyone personified the new historical trend in classical music, himself co-edited Couperin's complete works.

It's worth pausing to consider the oddity of that situation. Here was Liszt, the most famous man of his age, whose concert tours were like Roman triumphs, rejected from classical music – whereas a French Baroque composer, whose music had lain pretty well forgotten for a hundred and fifty years, was welcomed in. What were these mysterious features that demarcated this newly emerged classical music in the Western world from the rest of music? What is the quality that the musical world of the mid-nineteenth century found in the music of Couperin, a composer so stylistically removed from their own world, but could not find in the most famous musician of the era?

A short answer would be depth. But what measure could be used to fathom the depth of music? That has proved to be a massively contentious issue; but one way of defining depth in music is to say what it is *not*. As soon as the category of 'deep' was invented, its grinning shadow, variously named 'shallow', 'cheap', 'sensationalist', sprang instantly into being. Thus we have the beginnings of the discourse whereby truth and authenticity are defined against the commercial and the formulaic – a discourse that still determines the way we talk about value in music.

It is worth digressing for a moment to point out that not all popular music was held to be bad. Folk music was revered by the Romantics, who thought it was the authentic, unspoilt expression of a people's soul. But it had to be rural music. Urban music wasn't made by the *Volk*, it was made by that frightening thing the 'masses', which had an alarming propensity for socialism and strong drink. Their music was therefore bound to be corrupt. (This contempt for urban man bizarrely reappears a century later in Bartók.) In the twentieth century the fault of the 'masses', in the eyes of the middle classes, has been not so much political as aesthetic. The masses are easily duped, they meekly accept whatever commercial pap the entertainment industry throws at them. But the picture is complicated, because the middle classes don't want to be high-brow all the time. They like to be entertained too, and so there grew up a kind of middle-class popular music. It was distinguished by a technical sophistication which could rival that of the art music realm itself, and even share some of its materials. Gershwin's jazz chords rub shoulders with progressions straight out of late Wagner; Sammy Hahn's 'I'll be seeing you in all the old familiar places' is a Brahms inter-mezzo with words attached. One of the ways in which rock and roll rebelled against bourgeois popular crooners was by throwing out their technical baggage.

The fact that some of the features of this labori-ously constructed 'musical realm' could be found in Cole Porter – and Duke Ellington and Thelo-nious Monk – is more evidence that the things that make for depth in music do not make a tidy, mutually reinforcing set of qualities. On the contrary, classical music is riven with contradictions and tensions, which is what makes it so endlessly interesting. This becomes clear as soon as you itemize the claims of classical music for a special, uniquely valuable status. Among them are:

1. The aspiration already mentioned towards the universal. This shows how far classical music is a child of the Enlightenment – which in turn helps to explain why it is now under suspicion! Classical music can never answer to an aesthetic of cultural particularism; it aspires to be the voice of anybody with a modicum of training or experience in its language (that is quite a large caveat, of course). This is not to say that classical composers have not nursed nationalist sentiments – but not even an avowed nationalist like Wagner wanted his works to be understood and appreciated only by Germans. World redemption was his aim. Similarly the great Czech composer Janáček regarded the Bohemian accent of his music as bearing a universal message.

2. The dominance of the text. One reason Liszt wasn't welcomed into the canon was that his pieces were too obviously vehicles for

a particular charismatic performer, namely himself. This reversed the proper order of things. Classical music consisted of works, a set of pieces which could be reproduced anywhere, anytime. (This is a vast generalization which skates over the importance of improvisation in Baroque and Classical music. But by the Romantic era, the text had extended its dominance and squeezed out almost every vestige of performer freedom.) Performers were no more than their humble servants (Liszt claimed to be such a humble servant, but no one believed him). The existence of the text pointed to a distinction between the essence of a piece, the set of formal relations which were its permanent features, and the particular inflections those relations acquired in performance. It was the way classical music could be fixed in texts, which could then be stored in libraries (or sold in shops) that removed it from the corrupting effects of time.

3. Another aspect of the classical music that tended towards fixity was its rule-bound nature. To a degree, classical music is something that can be codified in the form of abstract rules, which can be written down in manuals. This puts it at the opposite pole to traditional musical practices, where musical authority comes from being a member of a certain family, or from studying with a guru

or master in a long apprenticeship that is as much ethical as musical. The skills of classical music, by contrast, can be acquired by anyone with the patience to master the techniques. Alongside the rational nature of the rules goes a bureaucratic form of organization. Classical musicians are not the keepers of the wisdom of the tribe, nor are they the vehicles for the 'breath of Apollo'. They are unionized professionals.

These are the aspects of classical music that pluck it out of time and place. And when people want to attack it as irrelevant, it's not surprising that it's these aspects they seize on. But there are other features of classical music, no less essential to it, which tend in quite the opposite direction. Two of them are:

4. Inspiration. This is the mysterious X factor that escapes the net of technique, the thing that no manual or conservatoire can give you. It is what separates the perfectly competent, but routine piece, from 'real' music which stirs the feelings and exercises the mind. Whether a piece could be both unimpeachably correct and inspired was a rich source of argument.
5. Constant change. Classical music is always being accused of being 'stuck in the past' and 'irrelevant'. And yet the most striking and

obvious fact about classical music is its colossal dynamism. It looks back, the better
to leap forwards. From about 1600, when
the secular spaces of the opera house and
aristocratic chamber took off, the pace of
change in classical music hots up, but it
doesn't become break-neck until the onset
of the bourgeois era (which of course was
precisely the moment when classical music
becomes aware of itself as a separate category of music). Through the late eighteenth
and nineteenth centuries stylistic evolution
moves faster and faster, leading eventually
to the cataclysm of modernism.

There's a whole set of tensions here, between
fixity and change, between rationality and irra-
tionality, between individual and type. They're
bound up with another tension, between music as
seen from within, and from without. When music
takes on a new sort of existence as a separate
realm – a realm made up of practices and ideas –
it becomes another item in the world, something
towards which each individual has to take a
stance. This shows itself at the simplest level as
appetite or indifference. We all know of people
who simply don't like music. But that simple fact
points to the peculiar status of music in the West.
In traditional societies, music cannot be a matter
of personal choice, because it never presents itself

as separate from one's own being in the world. There, music is constitutive of one's very being; the question whether one likes it, or understands it, is really neither here nor there. One doesn't approach music, one is seized by it.

There's another tension in classical music, one which has left its mark on the structure of this book. To speak of classical music as a realm implies that there is *one* key which will grant access to it. But the fact that it lies outside oneself, and is an object of choice, means that there can be no single, simple route to it. It can be an object of marvel, or pleasure, or suspicion, or curiosity. And of course one can participate in it (though most of us don't). This means that there are many keys to the realm of classical music, each of which opens a door to a place so different that you're not sure, at first, whether they really are in the same realm. There is the sociologist's key, which looks at music as a set of social practices. I avoid this one, for reasons I've already mentioned. There is the key of interpretation, the one which leads to a set of meanings. And there is the musician's key, the one that talks about the stuff of music, and the laws that bind it together. It's the second of these that I'll turn to first.

Phrases like 'musical material' or 'musical stuff' tell you something important. It tells you that music is made *of* something – it is made of notes (more recently it's been made of noises too, but let's leave that on one side for now). Notes can be joined in higher-level entities – melodies, harmonies, rhythms. These too can be joined up to make bigger things – songs, sonatas, symphonies, operas.

This notion seems so obvious that it's tempting to regard it as universal, a quality possessed by any activity one might think of as musical. In fact it isn't. In non-Western cultures, music is indivisible; it is created and received as a sounding whole. In that respect it mirrors the indivisibility of the social situation it is part of. The 'parts' of a Malian wedding song cannot be conceived separately, any more than the wedding can be conceived of without the song, or the song without the wedding.

Compare that to a piece of Western classical music, where the parts are indeed specifiable in isolation. The tune of the first movement of Haydn's 'Lark' Quartet can be hummed apart from that dryly hopping accompaniment, and still make sense. If the parts are independently specifiable, it must also follow that they are also substitutable, in the sense that bits of the music can be replaced by new bits that fulfil the same grammatical function. A different melody could be placed over that hopping accompaniment, or, conversely, one could keep that wonderful melody and compose a new accompaniment, which would make perfect harmonic sense. This is inconceivable in traditional music, where the concept of grammatical function is lacking.

Grammar implies rules, and rules have to be learnt. Traditional music too has its rules, but these are embodied in practices – they are not specifiable in abstract forms (thus the 'esoteric' quality mentioned above, whereby music becomes the possession of a musical caste). But where rules are abstract, and specifiable apart from any specific performing moment, they become democratic. They can be written down in manuals, which anyone can buy, or taught in conservatoires, open to anyone with a 'musical' ear and aptitude. Thus it was that, beginning in the eighteenth century and accelerating mightily in the nineteenth, music acquired an institutional framework which embodied the 'cultural space' of music. The educational element of this institution laid down the methods for constructing the 'parts' of music, and also taught the skills needed to play them.

Notice how a separation of functions applies to every aspect of this 'cultural space'. On the level of musical discourse, everything could be taught separately – harmony, counterpoint, analysis, orchestration. On the social level, the old role of musician fissiparated into numerous specialisms – choirmaster, composer, bassoonist, pianist, mezzo-soprano (as recently as Bach many of these functions could be combined in one person, though specialism was already emerging). Likewise the curious new feature of 'substitutability', manifested within the discourse of music, was replicated at the social level. Any orchestral bassoonist can be substituted for any other (they are 'fungible', like bank-notes) because the criterion of musicality is no longer a social one – belonging to the right caste – or charismatic –being touched with the 'breath of Apollo'; it is to do with the acquisition of technique.

Technique is a purely instrumental thing – it asks no awkward questions about the 'why' of something, only about the 'how'. The teaching of it gives rise to that curious thing, absolutely unique to the West; the technical exercise. Those dreary books of scales, finger exercises, 'schools of velocity' achieve something which is, in non-Western cultures, literally inconceivable; they separate the physical skills needed to play music from any conception of musical value or function. These exercises are repellent for the same reason sex manuals are grotesque; they treat technique as if it were a desirable attainment in itself.

The tendency to separate out technique and musicality is just as pronounced in composition. It is perfectly possible to write a fugue which obeys the rules laid down in one of those forbidding textbooks like Gédalge's *Traité de la Fugue*, and yet is poor as music. (These textbooks still haunt the shelves, and the syllabuses of conservatoires.)

Just as performing technique is something one 'applies' to music, bringing the dead notes on the page to vivid life, so techniques of composition are 'applied' to musical material, spinning it out, developing it, transforming it.

But not creating it. However impressive the technical armoury of a piece, there's always some bit of it, however small, which must escape technique. It is the *Einfall*, the Given, the spontaneous gift of the fingers wandering over the keys, or of the unconscious which sends it into the composer's inner ear. Where the given ends and technique begins is an impossible question to answer, at least in good pieces. It is one of the marks of a second-rate piece that the join between those things is so easily spotted. Franz Berwald's symphonies often begin with a wonderful spontaneous utterance, but soon you feel the dead hand of some mechanical procedure; a too-predictable harmonic sequence say, or a pattern repeated with all-too-evident regularity. Compare Brahms, where even the humblest linking passage has the mysterious inner pregnancy of a true inspiration, and every striking idea is simultaneously a triumph of technique.

Given that the material of music is always dual in nature, at once 'given' and constructed, we're bound to find that memory and convention, and formal patterns inhere in even the most startlingly original musical utterance. There can be no genuinely new-minted material, nothing that breaks every category. For example: to count as a rhythm, a series of irregular durations cannot be totally irregular. To speak of 'random rhythm' is really a contradiction in terms. There has to be, at the very least, a regular minimum unit, of which the larger units are instantly understood to be multiples. And probably there'll be a lot more than that bare minimum. There'll be a recurrence of small patterns, which provides a hook for the listener's memory, and those smaller patterns will be grouped into larger ones. And the patterns will not necessarily be neutral; they may evoke a cultural norm, like 'march' or 'reggae'. At the dawn of the modern era – which is where this chapter is leading to – the rhythmic repertoire of Western art music was filled with such norms. They didn't include 'reggae' but they certainly included march, and waltz. In purely formal terms the range of patterns was narrow; most music was in triple or duple time, and irregularity was a subtle matter of shifting accent and phrase length.

Rhythm, before the modern era, wasn't conceived as a musical category in itself. There are no rhythm textbooks, or conservatoire courses. Melody too was taken to belong to the realm of material rather than technique; in fact it was absolutely the favourite site for inspiration to strike. In Romantic music inspiration was felt to be basically lyrical in nature, just as it was in poetry. However, if melody were pure inspiration, it would appear new-minted along the whole of its length. But melodies are not like that. The fact that a typical tonal melody gives us the signs of self-identity – i.e. it contains smaller units which are repeated – takes melody into the realm of form. And if melodies have form, they become amenable to judgement on technical grounds. People used to talk of 'well-formed melodies'. The criteria for a well-formed melody are odd, in that they make no mention of the expressive or performative features, which you might think would be the ones that really count. They are to do with balance and symmetry. A well-formed melody typically consists of multiples of eight-bar phrases, which themselves can be subdivided into four- and two-bar phrases. The cor anglais melody from Dvořák's 'New World' Symphony is a good example of the type, though that folksy regularity makes it not altogether typical of its time. Late Romantic music favoured irregularity, and a spinning out of the lyrical impulse in a way inspired by Wagner's 'endless melody'.

Towards the dawn of the modern era, the expansion and loosening of melody went hand in hand with a dizzying expansion of harmony. Harmony was indubitably part of technique, sharing the limelight in that bugbear of countless generations of conservatoire students, 'harmony and counterpoint'. In fact the grip of technique was

tighter here than anywhere else, because it specified not just the means of getting from one chord
to another, but what the range of admissable
chords was. Any chord (at least, any chord that
was a genuine harmony and not a chaotic jumble)
could be labelled with a complicated system of
roman numerals and letters, showing how near
or far it was from the key-centre, what chord-
type it belonged to, and how far that type was
blurred in the particular instance by 'added notes'.
This complicated taxonomy, combined with the
'voice-leading' rules of counterpoint, allowed anyone to construct intelligible harmonic progressions. A progression that couldn't be explained
within the system would be judged incoherent, as
Schoenberg discovered in 1899 when Vienna's
prestigious music society, the Tonkünstlerverein,
refused to consider his *Verklärte Nacht* ('Trans-
figured Night') for performance because it contained a 'single uncatalogued dissonance'.

By the turn of the twentieth century, the tension between the increasingly wayward offerings
of inspiration and the technique that sought to
constrain and order it was becoming acute. In
time, the whole basis of the relationship between
those things would have to be rethought. Composers began to speculate about forms of music that
would allow the inner voice to run free, uncon-
strained by technique. Others had a wild vision
that was just as extreme, but in the other direction.

What if new sorts of technique could be devised that didn't need material to work on, techniques that would actually create a new, unprecedented sort of material, free of culture and memory?

But we're getting ahead of ourselves. First let's turn to the other side of that new musical realm, the side to do with meanings and values.

NOTES

1. Des Voeux, Sir G. W. (1903). *My Colonial Service in British Guiana, St Lucia, Trinidad, Fiji, Australia, Newfoundland and Hong Kong, with Interludes*. London, John Murray.
2. Agawu, K. (1995). *African Rhythms: A Northern Ewe Perspective*. Cambridge, CUP.
3. Robert, D. (ed.) (1998). *Lord Chesterfield's Letters*. Oxford, OUP.
4. Burney, C. (1967), ed. Frank Mercer. *A General History of Music*. New York, Dover Books.

2

❧

Words, Words, Words

There are many reasons for valuing music. Some are personal; we might feel a pricking behind the eyes at a Dire Straits song because it reminds us of a first date. Or it might be at the other end of the scale of human experience. We might treasure the closing pages of Stravinsky's Symphony of Psalms because it gives us a glimpse of what the religious experience might be like. But it's tempting to think that all the reasons for valuing music, lofty or sentimental, are grounded in the innocent pleasure of moving with the music, savouring its melodies, thrilling to its climaxes. These are the things you might be tempted to call 'purely musical', in the sense that nowhere else in life does one find experiences quite like them.

But the strange thing about these purely musical pleasures is that the moment we try to isolate them we're forced into the realm of metaphor. We're so used to talking about a falling melody, or a dark harmony, or an anguished chord, that it takes an effort to remember that mere vibrations in the air cannot be any of those things. Stormy music is not literally stormy, even though some philosophers have made strenuous attempts to argue that it is. But without metaphors like these, we wouldn't hear music, only sounds. That much is true of any musical perception not mediated by social action; we have to hear sounds *as* something (as the philosopher Peter Kivy puts it, we always hear music under a description).[1]

Once we admit that this kind of metaphorical hearing lies at the root of musical experience, that mysterious realm of the 'pure musical experience' – the Holy Grail for so many nineteenth-century writers on music, and quite a few modern ones as well – starts to seem very elusive, if not downright implausible. If we can't even understand a melody without importing extra-musical ideas like 'rising', 'falling', yearning', 'happy' and so forth, what chance is there of hearing an entire symphony in a 'purely musical' way?

In the view of many people, there is no innocent way of hearing music, and no purely musical experience. As soon as music is understood as music, it becomes a cultural fly-paper, attracting all kinds of meanings. Some of those meanings are attached to music from the moment of its birth. When a social form calls forth music to articulate it, the meaning of the music is entirely absorbed by its function, without any residue. A medieval dance like the *estampie* owes its intricate patterned form entirely to its social role, which is to co-ordinate the intricate patterns of the dance. Similarly, a piece of liturgical chant gets its meaning from the sacred text that it intones. No act of interpretation is required; we don't need to go burrowing into the composer's psychology to find out why the chant is in a minor key, even if we knew his name (which in most cases we don't).

Because the meaning of music before the modern era is entirely swallowed up in function, it never occurred to writers of the time that the meaning of music might be worth discussing. Look back to musical treatises on music from the medieval era, and you'll find endless abstruse descriptions of music's mathematical basis, nitpicking distinctions between consonance and dissonance, and speculation about the symbolic connection between music and the divine (the connection between triple time and the Trinity was often stressed). But the expressive power of music is dismissed in a few conventional phrases. In medieval France music was felt to be 'joyous', in fact the word *joyeulx* was often used as a synonym for music.[2] There's a similar conventional quality in sixteenth-century English sources, where music is summed up briskly as 'merie' or 'sad'. These conventional terms were really a way of saying that the music deserved the name of music. It had succeeded in its purpose, of being an aural embellishment which set the seal on an occasion, lifting it from the humdrum into the solemn or festive. It's not that people weren't alert to nuances of feeling and meaning; it's more that the nuances were given by the interaction of sound and context. Music was hardly thought of as a separate thing; it added a grace to something, like silverpoint on a Renaissance drawing.

But once music falls away from function, its meaning becomes open to argument and inter-pretation. And it becomes open to change through time. Of course, this is true even of music whose meaning was once fixed. An Elizabethan madrigal cannot be merely 'merie' for us; it will be overlaid with all kinds of new associations. These won't always be welcome; for me those 'fa-la-las' are hopelessly tainted by images of Charles Laughton in an ill-fitting doublet. You could say that's just my problem. But that's precisely the point. We all have private associations that we bring to music, along with all the interpretations dreamt up by the musicologists (particularly the so-called 'New Musicologists', for whom the whole idea of 'pure music' is a wicked bourgeois notion to be rooted out) and the change in perspective brought on by the passage of time. The slow movement of Mozart's E♭ major quartet now has a Wagnerian ring which it couldn't possibly have had for its creator, or its first listeners.

MUSIC: HEALING THE RIFT

The change from music as the ornament of an occasion to music as something to be contemplated and argued over could hardly be an abrupt one. The passage from one to the other was slow, stretching over centuries, and it was mediated by another form of existence, which you could call participation. Participation in music may be occasional in nature, but it doesn't have to be. In fact, the whole trend of musical participation in the nineteenth and twentieth centuries (at least as far as art music was concerned) was away from socially or religiously motivated forms of participation to new ones that were purely private. You get a clue to the high-minded tone of this newly emerging private form of music-making from the title-page of J. S. Bach's *Das wohl-temperirte Clavier* ('Well-Tempered Keyboard'), which states that the music is 'For the young musician who wishes to learn and for the pleasure of those already skilled'. *Clavier-Übung*, his large collection of keyboard works, is styled 'Keyboard Practice to Refresh the Spirit of Music-Lovers'. Pleasure needs work to sustain it.

This was the beginning of that vast change from music as something essentially public to something essentially private. Bach came at the beginning of the enormous upsurge in domestic music-making, which was utterly different in kind to the music-making that had always gone on at home – lullabies, folk song. This new sort was aspirational in its essence, involving the spending of hard cash on harpsichords (and later pianos), music lessons, and sheet music. It involved work – in the form of practice – as much as pleasure. And it could not rest easy with inherited repertoire – it had to be on the look out for what was new and fashionable. But blended in with the social aspiration was a cultural one. The presence of a piano in a nineteenth-century home was a sign of gentility. As much as the volumes of Scott and Ruskin on the bookshelves, it showed that the owners were keen to better themselves.

When music is an occasional affair, the question of what its expressive content should be hardly arises. But when it's set on the road to privatization, content becomes an issue. Again, the issue didn't become too pressing as long as bourgeois music remained a largely participatory affair. The content was created by a new social function, which was to bestow a sense of privacy. Privacy is an ambiguous word; these days it tends to be synonymous with solitude. But there is such a thing as a shared privacy, the privacy of the home. As mass society developed, the home became, for the bourgeois, a refuge from a hectic and threatening world. Music helped to create that private space. You could say that a large part of the content of the various domestic music genres – the salon piece, the song, chamber music – was domesticity itself, the sense of a delicious cosy intimacy. Even where the subject of the music appeared to be a storm (as in Tchaikovsky's 'The Seasons') or goblins (as in Schumann's 'Fairy Pictures') the subjects are as it were miniaturized, made safe, as if we're looking at them in a children's book (the tropes of 'domesticity' and the 'child's eye view' tended to blend into one another).

If private music inculcated a sense of privacy, one would expect public music to reinforce and articulate a sense of public space. The idea of a public space emerges, as you'd expect, hand in hand with the emergence of a 'public' music unattached to any particular function. Previously music had always been occasional, called forth by authority of some kind, religious or secular; just as there was no free and voluntary public realm to speak of, so there was no 'voluntary' public music. In the eighteenth century a new kind of public space arose which was in a sense permanent, unattached to particular occasions, and held in being by free-standing institutions like newspapers, learned societies, coffee-houses, and – among the most important – concert-giving institutions. Often these were combined – Bach's foray into this new 'public space' took place at Gottfried Zimmermann's coffee house in Leipzig, where he was the director of music.

But though music was an integral part of this vast social phenomenon, it also stood apart.

A newspaper can be read at any time, a coffee-house visited when one wants. But music in one sense is always occasional, in that it needs the co-operation of at least two people – someone who plays and someone who listens (leaving aside solitary musings at the piano). (Thanks to technology, the 'private' side of music these days vastly overwhelms the public side, with very curious consequences we'll come to later.) When larger numbers of people are involved, we have a genuine public event that has to be organized – a time has to be arranged, an appropriate space found, the appropriate musicians hired, advertisements placed in the newspapers, and so forth.

At one time, all these aspects of music's public being were imposed by the circumstances – which also determined the musical content. The time and place of a wedding were set first, and the musicians summoned afterwards: voices and festive instruments for grand weddings, voices and trombones for grand funerals. But in the new free public space of the emerging bourgeois, we have that very curious thing, a musical occasion with no 'occasion'. When the audience met at Zimmermann's coffee house to hear the fashionable Italian concertos arranged by Bach, there was no reason to be there except that they wanted to. This creates a problem, hardly solved today – who decides what the 'content' of this arbitrary 'occasion' will be? The other organs of the public world don't need to worry about their content – this was given by their function. There is always a fresh supply of news for newspapers, there was always some new theory or discovery to talk about at the Lunar Society in Birmingham or the Royal Society in London.

It took some time for the peculiarity of the situation to become apparent. The public concert at first simply borrowed its form, its manners and its repertoire from already existing musical resources. Church music was too solemn to drink and flirt to, folk music too vulgar; what the bourgeois really wanted was to be aristocratic, so forms nurtured at court, like the sonata and symphony, were taken over wholesale. For decades, centuries even, these forms carried the traces of their original social function, and its elevated social tone. The minuet of a Haydn symphony is an echo of a courtly dance; the Romantic horns in a Schumann symphony have, as their distant ancestor, the horn players at a court, who doubled up in the orchestra when they weren't out hunting. This determination to acquire aristocratic lustre went beyond the music; the Royal Philharmonic Society was in its early days keen to have real blue blood among its members.

But as the bourgeois class became more self-confident, it began to generate its own forms and tastes. Following fashion became as important as aspiring upwards, and what was fashionable was more likely to come from the musical world elsewhere than from the local court or noble house, which were now starting to seem distinctly old-fashioned. The 'aspirational' aspect of music if anything grew in strength, but it was redirected; it no longer aimed up, towards the aristocracy, but back, to the touchstones of value established at the outset of the bourgeois era. Music, in effect, developed its own aristocracy, a pantheon of composers who could at a distance be thought to have precisely that disdain for 'trade' and fashion that aristocrats were supposed to have. The myth of the 'poverty-stricken genius' sedulously culti-vated by the nineteenth century, is itself aristo-cratic; it is the mirror-image of the noble who is too refined to talk about money. Thanks to the myth, the real nature of a composer like Beetho-ven, who pursued fashion and the 'market' with systematic determination, was hidden until well into the twentieth century. Being, according to this myth, above fashion, the works of Bach, Mozart and Beethoven had a timeless value. That fact gave certain genres an automatic priority. Sonatas were bound to be serious, because Haydn and Beethoven wrote them; character pieces, how-ever original, just didn't merit the same respect (nor did their composers, as Robert Schumann discovered when he tried to marry the greatest concert pianist of the day, and found the father implacably opposed). Symphonies too were more serious than tone poems, for the same reason.

As the nineteenth century progressed (using that word in both senses) the tension inherent in the 'public space' of music started to become apparent. The inherited genres – symphony, sonata – derive much of their seriousness from their overtly public form of address. But the very idea of a distinctly public form of musical utterance was becoming problematic. The old forms, suggestive of grand ceremonial entrances, courtly dances, no longer seemed to fit the nature of these new public spaces, which were voluntary, animated by conversation rather than co-ordinated action, and entirely lacking in that sense of occasion that had always been music's life blood. The difficulty of defining a public musical space is vividly shown by the music that graced one of the few remaining 'occasional' public spaces, namely the church. In the nineteenth century church music quickly became archaic, not just because of its innate conservatism, but because the means no longer existed for summoning up a public space in contemporary musical terms. So composers had to have recourse to old ones; which is why the church, having been in the vanguard of art music for at least a millennium, now became a backwater.

The difficulty was – how to create a new form of public music that was more than just a remembrance of the past? The answer, discovered by Romantic composers, was to resituate the focus of attention and value in music. 'Moving with the music' now became a matter of following the music, making sense of it, explaining it to oneself and to others. To do this music had to become something it had never been before. It had to become expressive.

Expressive of what? is the natural question. There were two answers given to that question in the nineteenth century, each diametrically opposed to the other. They are best summed up not by nineteenth-century composers but by two modern ones. Igor Stravinsky and Arnold Schoenberg became the twin poles of modern music largely because they exemplified, and intensified, the two opposing answers to this question of what music's content consisted of. On the one hand, Igor Stravinsky, that ardent classicist and advocate of 'pure music', declared that 'music is, by its very nature, powerless to express anything at all'.[3] For him, music was about nothing except itself. Its only role, for him, was to create order in man's relationship to time – surely the most abstract kind of expressivity one could possibly think of. Against him, Arnold Schoenberg insisted that 'harmony is nothing but feeling'[4] – a claim certainly born out by his own music, which expresses the farthest reaches of feeling with the maximum intensity.

On a first glance, nineteenth-century music seems to bear out Schoenberg's view that music's aim was expressivity first and foremost. The galloping technical enlargement of music's domain, remarked on in the previous chapter, went hand in hand with a vast increase in the range and intensity of feelings that music could capture. But the change wasn't just engendered from within music's own substance. It was generated by composers determined to infuse music with expressive ideas and images drawn from outside music, above all literature. In the music of composers like Liszt and Berlioz, the alliance with the world of a certain writer becomes an integral part of the music's substance. One cannot imagine Berlioz apart from his literary gods, Virgil and Shakespeare. Liszt's image too is coloured by his literary allegiances: Lamartine, Goethe, Tasso.

The result of this cross-fertilization with other arts was a new sort of music. It no longer seized you bodily, enforcing a set of actions and thoughts; it sidled up to you, coaxed you, stirred up your feelings. Romantic music has that flattering quality, of appearing to address us personally. It has precisely those sudden surges, doubts, hesitations, forgettings, rememberings, fears and anticipations that we experience in our inner selves. This burgeoning inwardness became more and more the 'content' of private music; what is surprising is that it also became the content of public music as well. The peculiar power of Romantic music is that it can fill an entire auditorium with a vast, colourful, noisy simulacrum of subjectivity. The reason Wagner is *the* composer of the nineteenth century is that, more than any composer, he succeeded in reconciling the essentially private nature of the new Romantic musical language with a need for supra-personal resonance. On the one hand, he projects onto the largest scale a vision of the good life expressed in social terms. But using the same vast orchestral apparatus, and in the very same opera house of Bayreuth, he can focus on the merest tremors of the inner life. Nietzsche recognized this when he said that Wagner was 'our greatest miniaturist in music who crowds into the smallest space an infinity of sense and sweetness. His wealth of colors, of half shadows, of the secrecies of dying light spoils one to such an extent that afterward almost all other musicians seem too robust.'[5]

Opposed to this view of music as essentially expressive was the Stravinskian idea of music as essentially musical. The so-called 'formalist' notion that music's meaning is internal to itself was expressed most succinctly by Eduard Hanslick, music critic of the Viennese newspaper the *Neue Freie Presse*. He described music as 'the play of sounding forms', a definition which neatly evacuates music of any content. But Hanslick wasn't insisting that music was empty of meaning, in fact he was prepared to be as colourfully metaphorical as any other critic. It was more that music's meanings couldn't be translated into words. Mendelssohn agreed, saying that the real problem in describing music wasn't that its feelings were too vague, it was that they were actually too precise. Nietzsche too wanted to save music from its servitude to the other arts. 'Confronted with the supreme revelations of music, we ... feel, willy-nilly, the *crudeness* of all imagery and of every emotion that might be adduced by way of an analogy.'[6]

Wagner's take on this was bound to be different, determined as he was to forge the total artwork in which music joined hands with drama, poetry, dance and the visual arts. To be consistent, he had to believe that a philosophical or dramatic idea could fuse with a musical one. Even so, music retains a unique power: 'Music expresses the innermost essence of gesture with such immediate comprehensibility that, once it has completely filled our beings, it diminishes even the power of our sight to concentrate on the gesture, so that we finally understand it without even seeing it.'[7] But if we can't see it, how can we be sure it was there? It sounds as if Wagner is half-conceding the point that music constitutes a self-sufficient world after all. The musician in him had to concede that music's non-representational nature, the ambiguous nature of its signifiers, makes it the perpetual virgin. The other arts want to foist their meanings upon music, but it continually repulses them.

This tension in the conception of what art music was for wasn't just played out in the pages of the newspapers and philosophy books. It was evident in musical life itself, most sharply in Germany where anyone with an interest in music had to decide whether they were a 'Wagnerian' or a 'Brahmsian'. If you were a Wagnerian you believed music found its true consummation when joined to the word and the image, and you welcomed all the changes in the 'stuff' of music that helped it to become more expressive; more chromatic harmonies, ever larger and more colourful orchestras. If you were a 'Brahmsian' you were suspicious of all those things. You made do with an orchestra barely bigger than Beethoven's, you favoured classical forms like the sonata and the symphony, and good old-fashioned techniques like fugue, because these were what made music *musical*.

The problem with this idea was that it threatened to make music into something esoteric, something you could only understand if you were privy to music's 'secrets'. This problem only became acute in the latter part of the nineteenth century, as art music gradually moved beyond the capabilities of the amateur. In the time of Haydn and Mozart, and into the nineteenth century, art music's existence was a largely practical one. A typical middle-class music-lover would spend far more time playing and singing music at home than they would listening to it in the concert hall. The emerging canon of art music was spread to every corner of the Western world not through orchestral concerts, which for most people were inaccessible, but through keyboard arrangements, which anyone with some technique could play at home.

But as early as the second decade of the nineteenth century, when Beethoven's middle-period sonatas appeared, we can see art music moving beyond the capacities of the amateur performer. Later in the century, the rise of the charismatic virtuoso such as Liszt and Thalberg helped to intimidate amateurs still further. (One of the reasons for the historical bias of the canon is that Haydn and Mozart were less technically demanding than Liszt and Chopin, and so developed a tenacious 'after-life' in the form of arrangements slumbering in the piano stools of middle-class households, an after-life which lingers to this day.)

As music-lovers changed from active participants to passive consumers, their instinctive, lived contact with the new bourgeois musical realm started to wither away. If you're playing Mozart sonatas, you don't need to have sonata form explained to you. You can feel its contours under the fingers and in the nerves. But without that felt contact, music starts to become opaque, a trend exacerbated by music's tendency to become more private, more subject to extra-musical concerns such as narratives. The result is that, for the first time in its history, music becomes something that has to be explained to its users.

One symptom of that change is the rise of that peculiarly modern phenomenon, the programme note. Berlioz knew that unless audiences were warned in advance that his *Symphonie Fantastique* told a narrative of obsessive and doomed love, laid out in specific scenes whose content was partly scenic and active ('At the ball') and partly subjective (the recurring *idée fixe* representing the lover's obsession) the music would be largely unintelligible. That was why he furnished them with a printed synopsis for the first performance in 1830. But even when there was no ostensible 'programme' or narrative the need for explanations and aids to listening was felt with increasing urgency. Simply to present to an audience a series of musical sounds described with a bare generic label, say symphony, would no longer do, because the generic meanings were beginning to wither away. The real determinants of meaning were the individual features of *this* quartet or *this* concerto, put there with conscious deliberation by the composer.

As the locus of meaning shifted from generic markers to the individual features of a given work, the criteria of judgement shifted with them. The question was no longer 'is this an excellent example of its type?', but rather 'is this work meaningfully individual – is it the authentic expression of the genius of its creator?'. As soon as it was articulated, the dangers of this new aesthetic were sensed. Treating every work as if it were *sui generis* is strictly speaking an impossibility – there have to be some criteria of comparison, otherwise each work falls into complete solipsism. Judgement too becomes problematic, because at a trivial level every work is unique, unless it is an exact copy of another. Similarly with that other mysterious thing appealed to in the definition, 'genius', which links up in a dangerously circular way with the idea of uniqueness. Genius is untrammelled, scornful of conventions, and therefore produces unique works; any work which is scornful of conventions must therefore be the product of genius.

To guard against this circularity, the features of music had to be grounded in something objective. So it was that, alongside the 'picturesque' programme note – of which Berlioz's explanation of the *Symphonie Fantastique* is such a wonderful example – there arose that other form, which was a mixture of rather earnest moral appeal, and technical information. These told people how to listen, a strenuous business which went way beyond spotting correspondences between sounds and images. It was to do with following the music's grammar.

This concern for 'purely musical' values wasn't simply the nit-picking of professionals, anxious to maintain codes of practice in the face of ignorant enthusiasm of the public. It was more an attempt to embrace that public, and keep it within the 'realm of music' that was threatening more and more to become the province of professionals. The obvious route to that realm – through participation – was becoming closed off. The other route – the shared appreciation of music's new content, mediated by words – was a dangerous one. It ignored the very thing that made music special, its 'ineffability'. To the extent that music yielded willingly to words, and became a purveyor of images, stories, 'psychodramas', it wasn't really music at all, but a kind of aural aid to fantasy. Somehow the elaboration of music's content had to be conjoined with respect for its autonomy, which had to be given equal weight.

If the audience could be made to understand this mysterious dual nature of music, then to some extent the concert could become a true public event. Audiences would be lifted out of their subjectivity into the shared world of musical values, an objective world made up of techniques, rules, standards of excellence. Without that understanding, concerts would take on a schizoid character. On the platform the performers, relating to the music as music; down in the hall several hundred people drifting off into their separate dream-worlds. For musicians, and critics like Hanslick, dreaminess was the enemy. The great conductor Hans von Bülow insisted that music was about feeling – 'Gefühl' – and not 'Dusel' or dreaminess. Concert-going had to be part of the general effort towards self-improvement. John Ella, a concert promoter in London in the mid-century, promoted 'difficult' music such as the late Beethoven quartets for which he wrote detailed analytical notes. Appended to each one was a quotation from Baillot: 'It is not only the artist who must prepare for the public; the public must prepare themselves for that which they are about to hear.' Promoters in America were even more zealous in their educative mission; they sent out programme notes to subscribers in advance.

This strain of moral earnestness in nineteenth-century music was carried over into modern music. When Stravinsky toured the USA for the first time in the 1930s, several prominent newspapers published articles in advance of his visit, complete with music examples, explaining how this alarmingly modern music was structured, and how it should be listened to. By that time the need for programme notes had become even more acute, because the changes in music's material had accelerated way beyond the capacities of audiences to keep up with them. Come forward another 20 years, to the postwar avant-garde, and the relationship between music and its explaining text has become one of total dependence. Not a single feature of the music can now be 'taken as read' – absolutely everything has to be explained, from the nature of the sounds, to the 'grammar' that links them, to the guiding narrative idea of the piece.

The danger of this hypertrophy of explanation is that the relationship between music and the words that 'explain' it threatens to become inverted. When that happens, the music is judged according to how successfully it fulfils the programme note. This situation was noted as long ago as 1960 by the writer David Drew, who sarcastically suggested there should be an 'International Society for the Performance of Contemporary Programme Notes'.

But then so much in contemporary music seems like an exacerbation, or a parody, of trends born in the nineteenth century. Take for example the decline of genre, which was already becoming acute in the late nineteenth century. By the time of World War I, the idea of writing pieces entitled 'symphony' or 'sonata' had become passé; now music either bore a strictly neutral title that aroused no generic expectations, like Berg's Three Orchestral Pieces, or a unique one drawn from a scenario or a text. There was, it's true, a revival of the old genres during the neo-classical decades of the 1930s and 1940s, and of course in the Soviet Union the old bourgeois forms like the symphony were taken under the wing of the new proletarian aesthetic of 'socialist realism'. But after World War II genres were again banished by the second wave of musical modernists.

Another tension Romantic music bequeathed to modern music was the confusion between public and private. One of the reasons Erik Satie is such a prophetic figure is that he is the first composer in history to refuse, point-blank, the entire notion of public address. In the 1890s, at a time when Paris was succumbing to the orchestral and operatic plush of Massenet and Saint-Saëns, Satie was essaying a new enigmatic tone, sometimes mystical, sometimes comic, but always aloof. Even those pieces that are destined for large public spaces, above all the late ballets, simply mock those spaces by parodying the grand musical gestures that normally fill them. But his typical tone is emphatically private. One of his finest pieces, *Sports et Divertissements*, is actually impossible to perform adequately in public; its combination of silent texts (Satie was insistent that they should not be read aloud), calligraphy and music means that only the performer can really appreciate the piece. This emphatic refusal of a public rhetoric is found in a similarly extreme form in the music of one of Schoenberg's most gifted students, Anton Webern. And coming forward to our own time, what Nietzsche described as the 'miniaturist' strain in Wagner can be found in composers like György Kurtág, or Giacinto Scelsi, whose music is also made up of 'half shadows, of secrecies, of dying light'.

As for the newly subjective nature of music, that too threatened to run out of control. In the early years of the twentieth century, the pathological tendency in that new subjectivity, already discernible in Schumann (think of the strange disturbing irruptions of memory in pieces like *Carnaval*), becomes dominant. In the music of Viennese modernism, above all the works of Schoenberg and his pupils, the cosy privacy of Romanticism turns into agonized solitude. In the tiny chamber works of Anton Webern, just as much as in the nightmarish visions of a work like Schoenberg's *Erwartung*, the sense of a solitude become unbearable is the real subject matter of the music. It's no accident that that sense is so often expressed within a tiny frame – when the self becomes isolated, it shrinks to the tiny circle of its own obsessions.

But this is only one side of the story of how music became modern. It's the side that shows itself when we fix our gaze on the art music realm, with its own in-built tendencies to expansion and dissolution. But looked at another way, as something open to the world, that realm appears less gloomy. The story is then not so much a dissolution from within, as a sudden rude injection of energy and life from without.

NOTES

1. Kivy, P. (1989). *Sound Sentiment: An Essay on the Musical Emotions*. Philadelphia, PA, Temple University Press.
2. Personal communication from Dr C. Page of the University of Cambridge.
3. Stravinsky, I. (1975). *An Autobiography*. London, Calder and Boyars, p. 53.
4. Letter from Schoenberg to F. Busoni, quoted in Beaumont A. (ed.) (1987). *Ferruccio Busoni: Selected Letters*. London, Faber & Faber, p. 389.
5. Nietzsche, F. (1968). *The Case of Wagner*. Trans. Walter Kaufmann, New York, Random House, Section 7.
6. Nietzsche, F. (1968). *On Music and Words* (fragment). Trans. Walter Kaufmann, New York, Random House.
7. Wagner, R. (1955). 'Beethoven', in *Actors and Singers*. Trans. William Ashton Ellis, Lincoln, University of Nebraska Press.

3

❧

Things Fall Apart

Sometimes a musical tradition stands in dire need of that rude shock from outside. But in those cases, the arrival of the fertilizing new influence is no accident. It comes as the result of an unconscious seeking out, an appetite, as if the inhabitants of a musical culture are aware, at some dim level, that they belong to something tired, used up. It's hard not to see the rise of world-beat in the 1980s as an inchoate craving for something raw and vital in pop music, qualities that had hardly been seen since the days of punk.

Of course, there has to be that complicity between the host culture and the new arrival, otherwise cultures would never mingle at all. But there are degrees. Looking back to the arrival of the Other into classical music in the early twentieth century, the signs are more mixed. The desire for the exotic and the untamed is certainly a leitmotif in modern music, from Chabrier and

Debussy down to the present. But mingled with that desire is something you never find in today's pop musicians, insouciantly roaming Africa with their mini-disc recorders, gathering material that will soon work its way into their next album. Within classical music there's also a movement of rejection, or, if not rejection, a determination to hold this exciting and enticing thing at a distance.

This attitude is in fact the normal one – to us it appears peculiar, and even neurotic, only because we've become inured to the mind-set of world music, with its flattening, levelling ideology of universal welcome. But look back, and you find that encounters between cultures are fruitful precisely because desire and fascination are mingled with their opposite: an instinctive sense that the Other must be held at arm's length. And this movement of rejection, which might appear to be dismissive, is at bottom a form of respect. It acknowledges that this thing is indeed profoundly different, strange, possibly threatening – and not to be lightly taken on.

The attitude of the Western art music realm to the Other has – until very recently – always been of this sort. Like any musical culture, apart from the one we now live in, it has presented itself, to the people who participated in it, as an entire, integral whole; not one musical practice among many, but *music* itself. But there were particular reasons why this belief was tinged with both arrogance and insecurity. The practice of classical music no longer had that unarguable instinctive certainty that adheres to traditional musical cultures. It had become rationalized and institutionalized, and thereby taken into the realm of debate and argument. In traditional musics, a form of utterance either belongs or does not belong; there are no borderline cases. But once you frame a static set of rules, musical practice – which is always on the move – will be in a state of tension with the rules. Borderline cases will then appear. And the quicker musical practice mutates, the more those borderline cases will multiply.

On the other side, there were reasons why the self-belief of Western music should be especially strong, to the point of being overweening. By the end of the nineteenth century it had acquired a technical armoury which seemed to bring the whole of experience into its ambit. This was not the totality experienced when musical practices exist to enact an all-encompassing world-view, which is what we find in traditional musics. These forms of music achieve their wholeness by exclusion, by ruling other forms of musical experience out of court. That sense of music as a *plenum*, an all-encompassing fullness, also attaches to Western music, but in this case fullness is expressed, rather than enacted and lived. By the end of the nineteenth century, music had swept into every last crevice of subjectivity; there seemed to be no area of experience that wasn't subject to its magic power. And this was achieved through a vast expansion in music's technical means. Music had colonized the inner world through a form of technical mastery, just as engineering, technology and capital had mastered the outer one.

So it's hardly surprising that Western art music became domineering as well as exclusive. For a music-lover in Vienna in 1880, music was what he had in his piano stool, and what he heard in St Stephen's cathedral and the main concert hall or Musikverein – that was all. Or almost all. At a *Heurige* (beer cellar) he might hear some folk song which was too rude and rustic to count as music. But it was the voice of the people, a voice which had been ennobled through the works of Beethoven and Schubert (and so well ventriloquized by Mozart that melodies in *The Magic Flute* could actually become folk songs). So certain kinds of folk song could be allowed into music's antichamber, if not its temple. He might also hear exotic musics from one of the teeming nationalities of the Empire – Ruthenes, Croats, and of course Jews – playing in the pleasure gardens of the Prater, or the hardly less exotic sounds of regimental bands from different ethnic regions. And these, too, could be brought into art, though here the results were more controversial. Mahler's incorporation of military band music and Jewish wedding band music into his symphonies was greeted with distaste by the Viennese public.

This was one sort of borderline case. To be admitted to the sanctum of music, the folk had to be raised up to art, and the exotic thoroughly naturalized (the fact that we still refer to the process of acquiring citizenship as 'naturalization' is a reminder of how natural means – natural to us). The folk song *L'Homme Armé* (the armed man) has not the faintest trace of the street left when it appears in Josquin's two masses based on it – it could be a piece of Gregorian chant. The lute may have its origins in the Arab *'ūd* but we have to be informed of this. We'd never guess it just by listening.

These are examples of how different kinds of alien musical material – a melody and an instrument – could cross from the margin to the centre. It was a process that accelerated mightily during the nineteenth century, driven by increased mobility, new forms of communication, vast waves of migration, and the imperial adventures of the Western powers. These colossal historical forces produced, as an accidental by-product, innumerable musical encounters. At first these would happen far away from the centre, within the margins themselves. Sir William Jones took time off from his duties with the East India Company to investigate Indian music, and in 1792 published

On the Musical Modes of the Hindoos. But as the eighteenth century passed into the nineteenth, and on to the twentieth, these encounters came closer to home. Migration brought exotic musics onto one's doorstep; the arrival of the phonogram brought it over the threshold, into the home. Before World War I recordings of ragtime were already circulating among well-to-do homes in Europe, and the rise of radio in the 1920s brought it, and other musics, within reach of those lower down the social scale.

The reaction to these encounters, on the part of the Westerner born and bred within the Western musical realm, might be one of marvelling curiosity, as in Debussy's encounter with gamelan music, which he described as having a rhythmic sophistication that made our music seem primitive. But along with the fascination there was often a sense that the interloper had to be kept in its place. The attitude of the French composer Francis Poulenc was typical. He was no ivory-tower aesthete; he'd collaborated with Cocteau on witty absurdist ballets, and his marvellous songs are full of echoes of French popular song. But there were limits to his populism. Distinctions still mattered; the idea of 'breaking down barriers' was still a long way off. 'I do not mind listening to jazz while I'm in the bath,' he declared, 'but I find it quite frankly odious to hear it in the concert hall'.[1]

Some composers tried to turn their back on the invasion. But most came to terms with it, even if that coming to terms resulted in rejection. The story of the how the art music realm struggled to come to terms with this increasing hubbub of musical voices, pressing in on the middle classes from every side, is really the story of musical modernism, though it is not the usual narrative. The usual narrative, as exemplified in numerous histories of modern music, including Simon Rattle's TV series *Leaving Home*, is that the dynamic for the change was generated entirely from within.

The story goes something like this. The advent of musical Romanticism led to an enormous expansion of music's harmonic and expressive realm (given that expression was more and more located in harmonic devices, these two expansions are really one and the same). That expansion weakened the basic syntactic rules that hold musical discourse together, above all the hier-archical structuring of key centres round a ruling home or tonic key. The move away from the tonic happened increasingly early, so that it hardly had time to establish itself, and the music roamed so freely that the return to the tonic seemed more and more like a merely formal bow at the rules.

By the time we get to the piano preludes of Skryabin, or to Strauss's early operas like *Elektra*, the dissolution has gone one stage further, to the level of individual chords. It's not just that the key centres seem unrelated to any central key; the key centres themselves have vanished into a tissue of chromatic chords, moving, apparently, in obedience only to the composer's whim (*mon règle c'est mon plaisir* – 'my pleasure is my rule', said Debussy) or to the promptings of his subjective inner life, as in the case of Schoenberg's so-called Expressionist works. Freed from rule, the focus of harmony moved to the delicious or troubling momentary change. Music becomes, in works like Schoenberg's *Erwartung*, a sort of emotional seismograph, registering every passing fantasy, desire, and fear.

Fear and fantasy were things very much in the air round about 1912, as World War I loomed ('I hate this oily stinking peace; if only something would happen', said poet Georg Heym, a sentiment echoed by many artists and writers on both sides of the Channel). The result of this unbearable tension is portrayed as a kind of dual apocalypse, the collapse of European civilization mirrored by the collapse of musical grammar. Out of the ruins, the second wave of musical modernism arises, to do with new systems of composition, new musical means, new aesthetics.

It's no wonder people find modern music so gloomy, when they're told that the whole thing was born from the heads of a few neurasthenic Viennese. But we only have to think of Satie's

Relâche, Ives's *Holiday Overture*, Matisse's sun-drenched interiors, Stravinsky's *Ragtime*, Tinguely self-destroying machines, to know that modern art can express *joie de vivre*. And it's no accident that the musical examples of that joy are the ones that refuse to fit the narrative. They cannot be slung on a world-historical line connecting the agonized opening of Wagner's *Tristan* with the agonized opening of *Erwartung*. For them we need a different narrative, one that has no need to invoke subjectivity or grammar, that has to do with curiosity, delight, serendipity, amazement – in short, with those encounters at the margin of music.

It turns out that the two narratives are really two sides of the same coin. The peculiar characteristics of the Western musical realm *c*.1900, the ones that made it amenable to expressions of fear, fantasy, dream, were also the very ones that made it hospitable to encounters. One of them has already been mentioned: the tendency within the system to indefinite expansion. In most musical cultures, change is driven from without, by encounters with other cultures. But Western music has a peculiar inner dynamic: it grows constantly, both in its material means and in its vocabulary. These two things go together; as Stravinsky pointed out, the orchestra expanded in the nineteenth century partly to accommodate the growth in available harmonies.

As the century progressed, new chords arrived in swarms – added sixths, the ninth, eleventh and thirteenth chords, augmented triads, whole-tone chords. Where did they arrive from? To say, from the unconscious of the composers, is to raise the 'unseen hand' in different words. To say that they were stumbled on by accident, as the hands wandered over the keyboard, is nearer the mark. 'Stumbled on' implies both novelty and familiarity. There has to be a sense of recognition, a sense of 'yes, this chord I've just discovered is the chord I want'. But this mysterious, and wonderful conjunction relies on a peculiar formal feature of Western harmony, possessed by no other system. It is really two systems in one – the narrow one of tonality, which is rule bound, and the neutral grid of the total chromatic that surrounds it. This larger space, which embraces the smaller one, is like a lattice of points, within which an infinity of lines can be traced. Any familiar chord therefore has two aspects – it has a historically defined name, and role, within tonality – say, 'the minor triad'. But it is also one of the infinite number of patterns traceable within the larger lattice – a lattice which is no theoretical construct, but is given as a sensuous reality every time a composer sits down at the piano keyboard. (This is why the piano is so much more than an instrument – it is the chief motor of Western music's dynamism.)

An example shows how this sensuous presence of something abstract can lead to one discovery after another. Play a G major chord at the piano – its solidity and stability (or, if you prefer, its dullness) tell us we're safely within the narrow space of tonality, in fact we're at its dead centre. Now add the seventh above (F) – already the sound is more flavoursome, and more dynamic. Pile up three more thirds by adding A, C and E and we have a thirteenth chord a sonority which is tangy but still safely within the tonal ambit. Flavour hasn't yet destroyed grammatical function. If we now keep that chord and push the C up a notch to C#, something mysterious happens. Function becomes blurred (that's to say, it isn't clear what chord should follow or precede it). But something is added. The chord suggests, all by itself, a very particular musical style. It's the characteristic sonority of late 1940s-style jazz known as bebop.

It is only when a harmonic practice reaches a peak of elaboration that a single chord could mark out a stylistic ambit, or even (in the case of the 'the *Rite of Spring* chord') a single piece. Notice too that when a single chord signals an entire idiom, or a single piece, we're on the threshold of dissolution. Just around the corner from the *Rite of Spring* lay atonality; and bebop paved the way for atonal 'free jazz'. These apparently unprecedented

chords were always there *in potentia*, just waiting to be made actual – just as the diminished
seventh chord, the favourite scary chord of silent
movie music, was lurking within the musical
fabric of Baroque music, and needed only to be
'recognized'.

So Western harmony is not a given, like a fact of
nature. It's a constant 'coming into being', as new
chords are plucked out of the ghostly realm of the
potential into the realm of the actual, when a
composer's hands stumble across them. The old
chords stay alongside them, so the net result is an
accelerating expansion. This ability of a musical
system to beget novelty from within its own substance, rather than through contact with something outside itself, is also found in jazz – one very
important reason why jazz might be thought of
as a species of 'classical music'. The expansion
of the harmonic resources of jazz between the
1920s and the bebop era went at a dizzying rate,
comparable to classical music in the previous
half-century, and it happened for much the same
reason. By the mid-1920s, the piano had become
as central to jazz as it had been to classical music,
and it's the peculiar way the piano keyboard gives
sensuous immediacy to something abstract – the
total chromatic – that makes it the engine of
progress in jazz too.

No wonder the illusion grew up that the
resources of musical grammar could engender a

musical revolution all by themselves, and that the only thing required to set this 'logic of discovery' into hectic motion was the tormented subjectivity of Arnold Schoenberg, Scriabin, *et al*. But the very formal factors that make the system so amenable to novelty from within also make it hospitable to invasions from without. The grid of the total chromatic is also a vast net, capable of catching any stray elements from outside. But however the encounter happens, the stranger always has to be 'naturalized', made fit for civilized company. The 'net' is no neutral thing after all, but rather a mechanism for engorging exoticisms and converting them into its own substance.

Viewed this way, the system seems coercive rather than hospitable. It doesn't allow for microtonal inflections found in so many non-Western musical cultures. And it's uncomfortable with music that has no harmonic implications. Before the modernist era, when tonality had not yet become an object of self-conscious worry, or rejection, it expressed itself through the choices of individual musicians in an automatic way, much as language 'expresses' itself through its speakers. And the unthinking response of the system to the grammatical solecisms of the Other was simple – they were expunged. The 'Hindoo' airs collected by Sir William Jones were supplied with keyboard accompaniments; in the following century, similar accompaniments were invented to neutralize the disruptive modality and rhythmic pungency of European folk song.

This domineering attitude worked well as long the 'the Other' was at a safe distance. But once it was on the doorstep, or over it, it became hard to distinguish its siren, worrying voice from the promptings of subjectivity; the inner turmoil was mirrored by – or perhaps one should say engendered by – the cultural babble without. Against this turmoil stood the system, comforting in its orderly behaviour. The problem, though, was that the system's magic power to assimilate all comers seemed to be failing. It had dealt with the Slavonic elements in Dvořák without too much trouble; it had swallowed the exotic sharpened fourths and flattened seconds in Chopin and Rimsky-Korsakov without demur; the Spanishisms in Tchaikovsky and Chabrier didn't disturb the smooth running of tonality.

It was very much disturbed, though, by the parallel fifths, pentatonic scales and flattened second degrees of Javanese gamelan music. Again, the reason for this disturbance was as much to do with social and historical reasons as with internal, 'grammatical' ones. The Parisian audience that heard Chabrier's cod Spanishisms in his 'España' weren't troubled by the gap between the source and the arrangement, for the simple reason that they had no opportunity to hear the former. With gamelan, and with other exotics like jazz, it was a different matter. It was now a generation or so after Chabrier, and the alarming and enticing features of the invader were right there, in all their unassimilated rawness. A 'harmonized' version of the Javanese gamelan was no longer an option when the real thing could be seen and heard in Paris (as it was at the World Fair of 1889, and increasingly often thereafter). Debussy was intoxicated by the sound, and tried to capture its essence in his piano piece *Pagodes*. The very title, which names a specifically Chinese cate-gory only to summon a sense of something vaguely south-east Asian, betrays an 'orientalizing' mind-set, but the disturbing effect at the musical level is profound. Familiar Western idioms – virtuoso 'impressionistic' decoration, the gravitational pull of the tonic, the very idea of an illusion of one sound-world generated through the means of another – all these enter a mysterious conjunction with genuinely Eastern elements, notably the pentatonic scale.

Debussy's piece shares its mood of unbroken tranquillity with a whole wave of 'orientalizing' pieces such as Délage's *Quatre Poèmes Hindous*, which posit a timeless East. (India is always being rediscovered by Western music, as the new enthusiasm for Bollywood makes clear.) The arrival of Indian idioms into the Western concert hall aroused no anxieties about a threat to Western tonality, perhaps because India was still at a safe distance. Jazz was more threatening. It had none of the apparent passivity of Indian music; it was infectiously rhythmic, it was associated with loose living, and it had the dangerous quality of being both absolutely modern (because it came from America) and absolutely primitive (because it was black).

It wasn't just fascist and Nazi ideologues who found jazz 'retrogressive' and barbarous. Many left-wing intellectuals and musicians were appalled by jazz's hedonism and the threat that white classical music culture would be swamped by 'niggerdom'. The British left-wing musician Casey Hampson, answering the question 'what is socialism', replied: 'In art it means that Bach, Beethoven, Mozart, Bantock and Boughton shall take the place of coon cacophony, cakewalks, rag and bone time and jazz.'[2] The dislike of jazz wasn't motivated solely, or even mainly, by racism, because the scorn of these defenders of high art was directed as much at the white audiences that loved jazz as the black musicians that made it. The animus against jazz was part of a wider distrust of the 'mass-mind' and 'mass-culture' that was a key component in the modernist mind-set.

You see this mind-set exemplified even in those forms of modern music that seem democratic on the surface. Charles Ives's music might seem to be the perfect expression of the American melting-pot, in the way it flings together marching band tunes, hymns, square-dances, in an exuberant, almost chaotic aural collage. But as Lawrence Kramer points out, black music is marginalized in this apparently democratic space, and by the end of these pieces a musical order is restored which 'affirms a social order that is rural, white Protestant, patriarchal and premodern'. In his essay 'The Majority' Ives advocates a democratic social space of 'free and unrestricted intercourse in all transactions . . . but it has to be governed by the Universal mind, the majority', set against the 'hog-mind of the minority'.[3]

Ives exemplifies one form of negotiation with the margin, which could be labelled 'rejection under the guise of assimilation'. But there were, at around the same time, less anxious and more joyous forms of assimilation. To many composers in the 1920s, jazz's connotations of modernism, untrammelled instinctuality and populism were wholly welcome, because they fitted perfectly with the populist ideology of post-World War I art and music. Jazz found some strange bedfellows – in Satie's *Parade* it joins hands with Dada, in Milhaud's *La Création du Monde* it melds with a primitivist evocation of a mythic landscape.

But again, the relationship is complicitous one. For these composers, jazz appeared, magically, just at the moment it was needed. In the period around World War I, Stravinsky's style was moving away from a picturesque Russianism towards a more lean, abstracted kind of modernism. But this most style-conscious of composers could never work in an entirely abstract idiom. He needed the dress of an idiom that would tear him away from Russian imagery, and encourage just that use of blurred-octave, major-minor dissonance and displaced metrical accent to which his instinct was leading him. And what better dress than ragtime, which could already be seen to have those qualities (at least, when viewed through the strongly distorting lens of Stravinsky's own personality).

But again, notice how, even in an apparently open and adventurous composer like Stravinsky, welcome is balanced by a certain distance. His jazz pieces are few in number, and their 'jazzy' features are quite superficial. Apart from the Ebony Concerto, written for Woody Herman's band, their scoring is as much classical (or Stravinskian) as they are jazzy. And they lack the most essential element of the jazz idiom, improvisation. This had to be so, because by this date, improvisation had been banished from art music (apart from a few isolated pockets) for a good century. In any case by the 1940s, when the Ebony Concerto was written, jazz no longer had quite the *frisson* it once had for classical composers, as it was well on the way to becoming 'classical' itself.

Having dipped a toe into jazz, Stravinsky quickly withdrew it, as did those other composers who essayed a jazz manner – Ravel, Milhaud, Martinů, Copland. This was bound to be so, because these composers couldn't go further into jazz without threatening the integrity of the classical enterprise. Stravinsky's numerous other stylistic borrowings were in a sense safer – and more successful – because they came from sources which were themselves classical, sources which ranged from Bach to his own contemporary Anton Webern.

Some composers refused even this cautious engagement with the popular or the exotic. Search the entire output of Schoenberg, and the only trace of the street you'll discover are the songs he wrote for the Überbrettl cabaret in Berlin. The numerous evocations of the waltz in the modernist works of Schoenberg (and in those of his pupils Anton Webern and Alban Berg) hardly count as popular music, as the waltz by that date (the 1920s) had only a twilight existence, having long since moved from the dance-floor to the concert-hall. As for up-to-date dances like tangos or fox-trots, there's no trace of them. More than any other composer, Schoenberg reveals the aristocratic tendency in modern music (though Stravinsky isn't far behind). Like Ives he was suspicious of the 'hog-mind', which for him was simply the majority; true value could only be discerned by a minority of cultured people, a minority in which blue blood could get someone an honorary membership, as his obsequious letter to Prince Egon Fürstenburg proves.[4] Schoenberg exemplifies the neurotic aspect of the classical tradition, which aims at purity, and erects barriers against unwelcome invaders.

In the early 1920s he invented a foolproof method for protecting that purity. The so-called 'twelve-note' or 'serial' method is usually portrayed as an attempt to put music's internal realm in order, replacing the now enfeebled grammar of tonality with a tough new one, strong enough to subdue all these obstreperous new chords. But it could just as easily be read as an attempt to keep out intruders. It achieves this by effectively banishing inherited memories and social idioms from the creative process. The basic unit of a 'twelve-note' piece is not a familiar category like a tune or a harmonic progression; it is an abstract ordering of the twelve notes of the chromatic scale, specially devised for each piece. This row becomes the stable source of identity in the piece, taking the place of the old key-note. A row is not dreamt up, nor can it be discovered by the hands wandering over the keyboard; it is carefully constructed, with a view to its long-term possibilities.

This means that the unconscious echo of popular idioms, which is normally an inescapable part of the creative process, is stifled before it can begin. I don't mean to suggest that Schoenberg's twelve-note music has no connection with the past; on the contrary, works like the Suite and Serenade are full of echoes of Brahms, of Bach, and of the *alt-wienerische* waltz. But it's notable that these are absolutely the only echoes the music allows. There's no hint of anything as mildly exotic as Bohemia, let alone India or jazz. It's as if Schoenberg has taken Eliot's observation that 'great creators choose their own forebears' and made it into an iron necessity. His method, as he used it, installs a lofty Austro-German pedigree for twelve-note music by a kind of *force majeure*, eliminating any other source of reference.

Later composers have tried to prove that this crippling weakness of twelve-note music is not so crippling as it appears. There have been numerous attempts to inflect Schoenberg's way of thinking with the old tonal means of organizing music, by composers as various as Alban Berg and Luigi Dallapiccola. And Stravinsky made an ingenious and surprisingly successful bid to marry Schoenberg's method with his own very individual harmonic sense. There have even been attempts to write twelve-note jazz, by Gunther Schuller and others. And there is the whole after-life enjoyed by the twelve-note method after World War II, when it was taken into new regions undreamt of by its creator, and in the process renamed 'serialism'.

MUSIC: HEALING THE RIFT

This has been the harvest of one response to the problem of how to preserve a distinctively classical form of music, in the face of all the pressures tending towards its disintegration. It's hardly negligible, certainly not as negligible as the fierce critics of serialism maintain. As for the flirtation approach of Stravinsky or Milhaud, that's always with us. Unlike flirtation in real life, these musical encounters always turn out to be risk-free, leaving hardly any trace on the creative biography of the composer who indulges in them, or on the developing history of the art form.

By contrast Kurt Weill's engagement with popular music was highly risky, involving a courageous move away from the high-art milieu he'd been raised in. The man who started out as a composer of astringently modernist music, a pupil of Ferruccio Busoni (who insisted, like Schoenberg, that true music was elitist in its very essence), became an advocate of music for the masses. During the 1920s and 1930s he composed radically politicized music-theatre pieces such as the *Threepenny Opera* which blended neo-classical traits with the sardonic tones of German cabaret. In the 1940s, after his emigration to the USA, he had to mollify his style, and his left-wing convictions, in order to succeed on Broadway. But whether or not Weill 'sold out' to commercialism in his American years (an accusation that still dogs his reputation) one thing is certain: all his music, from the early indubitably high-art Violin Concerto to a Broadway show like *Lost in the Stars*, stays securely within the ambit of the bourgeois musical world. It's a pretty safe bet that if Weill had lived to see the era of rock and roll, he would have abhorred it.

Alongside rejection and assimilation, there was a third way the art music realm could interact with the Other. What if, instead of engorging the Other to itself, art music allowed the invading music to suggest a whole new way of organizing its own substance – so the ruler becomes the ruled? This did in fact become a hugely important facet of contemporary music; but only where the encroaching music was of a particular sort. The exterior threat to the musical realm was really two-fold: it came from below, in the form of popular music, and it came from far away, in the form of non-Western music. (Jazz of course was both, which accounts for its pre-eminent status amongst these invaders.) But only the latter sort could be grist for this particular mill. One of the reasons contemporary urban popular musics are hard to reconcile with the art realm is that their organizing principles are purely *ad hoc*. There is no way that a jazz standard, a cabaret song, or a tango can yield anything of interest to a mind in search of some alternative ordering principle in art music, one that might, conceivably, be a substitute for tonality.

But look further afield, to distant classical music cultures, or even distant folk cultures, and you do indeed find novel formal features, used perhaps in an unconscious way. These could be as it were ennobled, raised to consciousness, by inter-marrying with the formalist aesthetic of classical music. This was exactly the fate of Balkan folk music when it encountered the fiercely formalistic imagination of Béla Bartók. Bartók was one of the great pioneers of musical field-work, writing down folk songs from the remotest regions of Central Asia and Turkey, and recording them on wax cylinders. Even before World War I, this vast enterprise was starting to rub off on his own music, but it wasn't until after the war that it became more than a picturesque element pasted on to a basically post-Romantic idiom.

The effect, ultimately, was to transform Bartók's music at its roots. It was ready for such a transformation; Bartók wrote that it was folk music which freed him from the tyranny of the major-minor system. But which came first: the perception that the major and minor modes were tyrannical, or the discovery of an untapped source of music that would help to overthrow them? Cause and effect are hard to disentangle, as always in these complicitous cultural influences; though there are reasons to think it wasn't so much the major-minor system Bartók found irksome, as the dominance of Austro-German music. Like

Janáček in Bohemia, Bartók was caught up in the surge of nationalist sentiment that was by then threatening to break up the Austro-Hungarian Empire. When he looked closely at the folk music he'd notated and recorded, Bartók found the germ of a different kind of logic, one which could prise Hungarian music away from Austro-German music, and raise it onto a supra-national plane of international modernism.[5]

The example of Bartók shows what a complicated and ironic tangle of forces went into the creation of musical modernism. How strange, to see a cosmopolitan musical modernism joining hands with Hungarian nationalism; stranger still, to see the discovery of an ancient 'uncorrupted' folk music as a way forward to the modern (though of course the conjunction of the primitive and the modern is familiar one in art of the period, above all Picasso). There's a similar conjunction in Stravinsky, whose Russian period leads, step by step, to an abstract modernism – and then, by another unexpected reversal, to that cool, detached playing with styles we now call 'neo-classicism'. It is the complexity of the historical roots, as much as the sophistication of the musical material, which makes twentieth-century art music so endlessly fascinating.

But viewed another way, the ironic complication of modern music is its problem, because it constitutes a threat to the unity of the musical realm. Unity – of practice and of expressive in-tent – is for these composers still a given, or what the philosopher Collingwood called an 'absolute pre-supposition'. The postmodern delight in frag-mentation was still a long way off, though some people want to see Stravinsky's constant changing of styles as postmodernism *avant la lettre* (though to my mind this smacks more of a desire to find a noble forebear for postmodernism – which heaven knows stands in need of one – than any real appreciation of Stravinsky's music).

That absolute presupposition is expressed in the fierce determination of these composers to meld the conflicting forces into a kind of willed unity, through the compelling force of a new musical logic. In the case of Bartók, folk music suggested a different way of organizing pitches and rhythms. Instead of being confined to a regular procession of three or four beats, so neutral that it becomes merely the grid on which the music is hung, rhythm (or rather metre) now moves centre-stage. Bartók's music dances and lunges in constantly changing beat-patterns, generating an excitement both mental and physical. As for the notes them-selves, they tend to cluster round a central axis, rather than some all-important key-note or chord. Or if there is a sense of gravitational pull towards a key-note, it will be distributed between a pair of notes, separated by an interval deliberately chosen so that neither can assume a dominance.

Bartók's approach to the Other is one of active seeking out; Schoenberg's is one of rejection; Stravinsky's is an attempt to turn the Western tradition into an Other to itself, treating its forms, its manners and its vocabulary with the same delighted sense of discovery as an ethnomusicolgist might treat Vietnamese court music. They were all successful, to a degree. But that success itself could not be anything more than partial, controversial, and ironic (I apologize for working that word to death, but it is the key-word of new music). Yes, there are masterpieces among these composers' mature works; but how many of them (particularly when it comes to Schoenberg) have found a place in the affections of the Western middle class, which is after all the heartland of classical music? Few, if the programmes of concert halls are anything to go by; fewer still, if one's measure of success is what people play at home. Only the boldest amateur string quartets play Bartók, fewer still play Schoenberg's Fourth Quartet.

And yet, there is a majestic quality to this body of music, which it ought not to have. Why is it that these three composers, and a handful of others – Janáček, Debussy, Ravel, Berg, Shostakovich, Britten – loom over contemporary music like giants? It's tempting to think, when one feels their giant presence next to the often smallseeming products of today's composers, that genius has fled the world, and that we live in a time of mere talent. Of course one could say that the appearance of giant size is, so to speak, a mere trick of the light; as these composers recede in time, their shadow gets longer. But there is a truer, more substantive reason. The music of these composers has a peculiar energy, a peculiar force, because they stand on the cusp between music as a unified realm, and music as a collection of fragments. One feels, even in the most rebarbative works of Schoenberg and Bartók, an echo of the lived unity that Western art-music once was. But mingled with that vanishing unity is a new sort. The future the music beckons towards is not anarchic; it has a new coherence which may be instinctive and empirical (as in the case of Debussy) or systematic (as in the case of Schoenberg and his pupils). It may come from within (Schoenberg again) or it may come from the shock of discovery (as in Bartók and Janáček's intoxicating discovery of folk music, or Debussy's encounter with the gamelan, or Milhaud's encounter with Brazilian music). And in each case, the new ordering sensibility or system is complicitous with the one that is vanishing. Listen closely to Schoenberg's 'twelve-note' works, and you hear the ghost of the old voice-leading rules, and rather more than the ghost of old forms like sonata form. Bartók may have resented the tyranny of major and minor at one level, but his new grammar never entirely supplants them, indeed in his late works of the 1940s they make a vigorous comeback.

That lingering trace of the old unity is what gives these works their peculiar vividness and authority. But they only have those qualities when approached as musical experiences. The instant you treat them as models of a potential new musical realm, to be emulated in practice, the uncomfortable truth about them – which one forgets as a listener, wrapped in a compelling aesthetic experience – suddenly becomes clear. They are partial, limited, touched by the arbitrary – and, to a degree, mutually exclusive. That is why we cannot stand on the shoulders of these giants; we can only look up at them from below, in bafflement and envy, knowing that the fate of music in our day is to be irredeemably multiple.

NOTES

1. Poulenc, F. (1935). Radio talk 'Mes Mâitres et mes Amis', quoted in Wendel, Hélène de (1991). *Echo and Source: Selected Correspondence of Francis Poulenc 1915–1963*. Trans. Sidney Buckland, London, Victor Gollancz, p. 382.
2. Hall, D. (2001). *A Pleasant Change from Politics: Music and the British Labour Movement between the Wars*. Cheltenham, England, New Clarion Press, p. 156.
3. Quoted in L. Kramer (1995). *Classical Music and Postmodern Knowledge*. Cambridge, CUP, p. 185.
4. 'The splendid enterprise in Donaueschingen [a contemporary music festival supported by the prince] is something I have long admired: this enterprise that is reminiscent

of the fairest, alas bygone days of art when a prince stood as a protector before an artist, showing the rabble that art, a matter for princes, is beyond the judgement of common people ...', quoted in Stein, E. (ed.) (1964). *Arnold Schoenberg Letters*. Trans. Eithne Wilkins and Ernest Kaiser, London, Faber & Faber, p. 108.

5. Frigyesi, J. (2000). *Béla Bartók and Turn-of-the-century Budapest*. Berkeley, CA, University of California Press.

4

Multiplicities

In 1907 one of the great symbolic meetings in music took place. Jean Sibelius and Gustav Mahler, the world's most renowned living symphonists, met during Mahler's visit to Helsinki and compared their vision of what a symphony should be. Sibelius said that he admired the symphony's style and severity of form, and the profound logic that created an inner connection between all the motives. Mahler's view was just the opposite. 'No!' he said, 'the symphony must be like the world. It must be all-embracing.'[1]

But where did the conversation go then? It's hard to believe that two such subtle minds didn't realize that these two views aren't necessarily contradictory. One can imagine a music that is impeccably unified, and yet full of expressive variety; it could even be 'impure' in its materials, if they were chosen and handled in a way that connected them to the germinating idea. And the converse is certainly conceivable. A composer could begin by assembling all kinds of 'found' material, folk song, dances, non-Western or whatever, and then set out to discover – or invent – a set of formal connections between them.

The truth is that given the date of this conversation – well before postmodernism was even a gleam on the horizon – it could equally well be interpreted as two ways of saying the same thing, rather than a stark disjunction of opposites. After all, Mahler doesn't say that a symphony is simply a neutral frame into which all and any material could be poured. He tells us that a symphony should compose a *world*, and a world must be perceivable as a singularity; there must be an order underneath, or above, the immediate appearance of chaotic exuberance. Which is exactly what Sibelius tells us, except that for him unity is the point of departure.

The question as to whether music should be singular or various, unified or disparate, is simply a recasting in formal, ahistorical terms of the question posed in Chapter 2: how were composers to deal with the bewildering arrival into music of the popular and the exotic? It is *the* question of modern music, which is why, despite the fact it took place a century ago, the conversation between Sibelius and Mahler is still the emblematic encounter of contemporary music. The question, apparently so simple, melts into ambiguity because at some level of description every musical utterance will seem various and complicated, while at another it will seem a model of simplicity. Interposed between them is the composer's intention, urging us to 'read' the music one way or the other. This may, as in the case of John Cage, be an urge to welcome multiplicity, and rule out any chance that it could be perceived as simple. But more common is the urge to unify and make a coherence out of what threatens to be chaotic. One way of doing that is to fashion musical utterances in such a way that their bid for coherence takes place on two levels; they project a unity at the formal level, but that unity depends for its persuasiveness on the other level, which one could call the projection of a singular vision, of the world.

This has become the guiding vision of musical coherence in much new music, which is why this chapter will focus on it. Before turning to it, it's worth glancing, for a moment, at other, less strenuous visions which identify coherence with a kind of primal simplicity. There are two routes to this simplicity, which one could call the historical and the formal. The historical route is the one favoured by totalitarian regimes, which is what makes it peculiar to the twentieth century. In aesthetic terms, both fascism and Stalinism are attempts to purge the complication and multiplicity that characterize the art music realm by the early twentieth century. They wanted to banish the modern, banish the intruders, and return music to a kind of purity, this state being represented by bourgeois art music just before it became tainted by the modern. It was an aim fraught with contradictions, because the bourgeois construct of art music was from the beginning tainted with complication; it could never hope for the unselfconscious unity of traditional musical practices. The response of aesthetic policy-makers in fascist Italy and Germany, and in Stalinist Russia, was to cleanse this taint by treating high bourgeois cultural forms (i.e. the symphony and opera of Tchaikovsky and Borodin in Russia, Wagner in Germany) *as if* they were something not formed by history but a given, like folk music. These would then become the vehicle for an aesthetic vision of a despotic purity; purged of their connection with real social life, they could become the passive vehicles of some ideal Utopian vision. And of course one of the defining features of Utopias is that they are pure, free of the complications of history, conflict, multiplicity.

The trouble with this idea is that it was precisely the historical dynamic coursing through high bourgeois music that gave it its vast power. It's the absence of that dynamic that accounts for a fundamental creepiness in music like the symphonies of Hans Pfitzner in Germany, the *Concierto de Aranjuez* of Rodrigo in Spain, the heroic cantatas of Prokofiev or Respighi's *The Pines of Rome*. However attractive this music, or heroic the rhetoric, it is at bottom a form of kitsch.

The other route to a primal simplicity – the formal one – couldn't be accused of kitsch; but only because it couldn't be accused of anything much. It's best illustrated by certain pieces written at the high watermark of New York experimentalism in the 1950s and early 1960s. LaMonte Young's Composition 1960 no. 7 instructs the players (who may play any pair of instruments, or sustaining keyboard) to hold the B below middle C and the F# above 'for a long time'. A recent performance by a string trio managed to keep this drone up for nearly 24 hours. Despite the appeals to Indian mysticism, hallucinogenic states, etc. that are routinely brought out to justify this kind of music, there is a bullying quality in this kind of conceptualism. No less than a Pfitzner symphony, it's an attempt to banish the complication of modern art and modern life. (Simplicity of this sort has in the past two decades lost its conceptual impetus and taken on an old-fashioned expressive turn, a subject I'll be turning to in Chapter 8.)

There's no getting away from it: simplicity, in the modern era, can never be innocent. Multiplicity is our natural state. But multiplicity too is a slippery term. If it refers merely to a large number of things, with no ordering or interpretative principle at work between them, then it's equivalent to chaos. And with one or two significant exceptions (again Cage comes to mind), chaos has not been the characteristic state of modern music (even though it may sometimes sound like it is). On the contrary, if one were looking for a single, sonorous phrase to characterize the adventure of modern music, it would be 'the hypertrophy of order'. How to order one's material, how to create a convincing sense of continuity, how to banish the spectre of the arbitrary that must lurk behind any music free of tonality; these are the obsessions of modern music.

This explains why those forms of technology that offer the unordered, 'chaotic' form of multiplicity have not been very successful. Take the invention of the Mark II RCA synthesizer unveiled in 1959 at Columbia University. According to its designers it could generate 'any sound, or any combination of sounds'. The language may be sober, but the promise of liberation by technology was intoxicating. Because of the limitations of 1950s technology, and a very defective understanding of the true complexity of acoustic sounds, the products of this monstrous machine, which weighed several tons and filled an entire room, were actually pretty limited. But the fundamental problem with the RCA machine was the purely arithmetical nature of the 'infinity' on offer. The 'new world' that it promised to open up was no world at all; it was a trackless waste, filled with meaningless objects, with no signs to distinguish up from down, beautiful from ugly, useful from useless. It was this, rather than technical obsolescence, which ensured that its career was short.

The really fruitful sort of 'multiplicity' is the one Mahler meant; the sort that composes a world. That requires some kind of ordering principle; but as we've seen, there were by the 1920s and 1930s several competing candidates for the best way to order music. But none of these captured the assent and loyalty of the art music world as a whole, let alone audiences. The result of that failure was that each composer felt obliged to work out his or her own salvation. And it was this free-for-all which led, by the 1960s, to that curious condition whereby each composer posits a form of music that is simultaneously a world-view. The best way to capture the peculiar flavour of this kind of musical enterprise is to look at a particular case. Here's Sven-David Ångstrom's own programme note for a work for a nine-piece acoustic ensemble with electronic 'real-time' transformation (an increasingly common mix these days), premièred at a new music festival in Germany a few years back:

Sven-David Ångstrom *Aporia 3*
This piece is concerned with threeness, particularly in connection with Thomas Aquinas's famous meditation on the Trinity in the *Summa*, and also by Marx's threefold

division of history into feudal, bourgeois and proletarian phases. Accordingly the musical material is imbued with threeness at every level; there are three instrumental groups, each consisting of three players, and their sounds are fed through a real-time digital transformation system based on three separate Fourier transforms. These are then fed into the auditorium via a three-channel system. The transition from one phase of these 'trinities' to another is fraught with 'aporia', that it is to say difficulties and hesitations, symbolised in my piece by placing Groups 2 and 3 behind a screen so they cannot see the conductor; Group 3 takes its cues from Group 2, and Group 2 from Group 1. Towards the end, we hear, through the speakers, a distorted echo of the Fred Astaire hit song 'Three Little Words', and also in the trombones, a quotation from the last line of Schoenberg's *Moses und Aron*: 'O Word, Word that I lack!' I dedicate my piece, with gratitude and admiration, to the Ensemble Suoraänliüu. Their constant striving for authenticity in a world of false, commercial idols is exemplified in their name, which means, in medieval Estonian, 'the striving that overcomes all obstacles'.

Well, I admit the première is only my invention. And it's true I couldn't quite resist the urge to parody. But it's a very mild parody; if you were to search the archives of the modernist music festivals like Royan or Donaueschingen you could find literally hundreds of programme notes very like this one.

The key question, of course is – what would my imaginary première actually *sound* like? How could those lofty ideological and philosophical ideas be given a musical reality?

To answer that we have to recall the basic distinction between sound and music. If one takes the view that these two things are the same, then of course the problem melts away, because the passage from idea to sound would be transparent. My imaginary but all-too-plausible composer could fashion a collection of sounds that projected 'threeness' in various ways – a three-part texture, say, or melodies having just three notes, or a harmony restricted to collections of three simultaneous pitches – and the audience could be relied on to 'read off' the message from the sounds. And many composers have behaved as if that is indeed the case.

But the passage from construction to perception, and thence to understanding, cannot be so simple. The old categories of music – melody, harmony, tempo, form – cannot be simply wished away. Audiences will always read those things into any collection of sounds, and if the sounds refuse to be read under those categories, audiences will reach the obvious conclusion, which is that what they're hearing isn't really *music* at all.

This stark fact has been eagerly seized on by the numerous conservative critics of new music. They see it as proof positive that the entire project of modernist music is a gigantic error, an error which now seems well on the way to disappearing into that sad limbo where the shades of the great failed ideas dwell, from phrenology to Marxism. Fortunately, it's not that simple. Alongside the swathes of empty pretentiousness which disfigure the face of new music, there have been profound attempts to rethink the 'realm of music' in the only way which has any real cultural value. Far from banishing the old categories, these new conceptions of music's realm reinvent them, in ways that connect the new forms with the old.

But to work, these new forms need a leap of imagination and sympathy on the part of listeners. Faced with these strange new sounds, they may not be instantly inclined to accord that sympathy; which is why composers have given them a helping hand. That helping hand comes, as I've said, from an infusion into the music of an imaginative superstructure, a world with which the new-old musical categories have an interestingly ambiguous relationship. That world supports the categories, but is also supported by them; it is both the vehicle of the music's substance, and that which rides on the vehicle.

To get an idea of how this peculiar symbiosis works in practice, let's look at a composer whose attempt to refigure music's old categories, and marry the resulting sounds with an entire worldview, has been brilliantly successful: Harrison Birtwistle. The instant you approach his music, you're aware that the experience is of a different order to encountering, say, a Haydn quartet, or even a quartet by Britten (though in the latter case one can see the beginnings of the need for a 'world-view' to support a musical argument). His pieces usher one into a world of compelling half-shades, a twilit world, imbued with a pagan sense of fatefulness and sudden, inexplicable violence. The peculiar tone of that world comes from its disparate sources; we encounter Greek sources (the Orpheus myth is a favourite), English archetypal figures such as the mysterious figure of fertility the Green Man, and the whole tradition of 'melancholia' as something precious, as portrayed in Jacobean poetry and the etchings of Dürer. Then there is his reverence for the aloof art of Piero de la Francesca. Alongside these is a fascination with natural processes of transformation, and with the way we perceive time (D'Arcy Thompson's *On Growth and Form* is a favourite book of Birtwistle's, and he's obsessed with time-pieces of all kinds). Linked to both those themes is another obsession: landscape, and the way it is articulated by perception (through the eye of both a roving and a static observer) and by collective action (processions and carnivals are constant sources of inspiration).

By themselves, these elements do not compose a coherent world; the connections are too obscure.

But the teasing way some parts of the picture cohere naturally, and others seem bafflingly separate, lends a portentousness to the whole. We look round for a key that will unite everything; and of course we find it in the music. And the reason the music has that magic power is that it takes familiar aspects of music – pulse, line, harmony – and reinvents them in a way that seems exactly appropriate for this world. Take the piece *The Fields of Sorrow*, based on a late-antique text by Pausanias about the Underworld, where sad shades walk by dark lakes. How right it seems that the setting should begin with a tolling piano octave, which is then bent out of shape; and that the cor anglais should wind around this obsessively repeated pitch, as if trapped; and that, towards the end, we hear piled-up repeated figures moving in deliberate rhythmic non-alignment, creating a beautiful musical metaphor for the twilit hopeless world of the poem. Of course any imaginative world worthy of the name must contain variety; and there are pieces in Birtwistle that explore the exuberant or violent side of his preoccupations, like *Endless Parade*, where his obsession with landscape and processions takes on a fierce, joyous tone. On the formal level, there is a similar congruence of musical substance and expressive intention. Birtwistle is obsessed by the circular patterns of myth, the way the same tale is retold with slight variations. But this is also an archetypal pattern of music, because recurrence and variation are indeed the primordial categories of musical form, which remain when the historical baggage of things like sonata and rondo have been stripped away. More genuinely novel is another favourite Birtwistle category, which one could call 'disjunction'. Here parallels in earlier music are on the face of it hard to find, but 'disjunction' is not so far from 'interruption' and 'separation', which have always been primordial musical categories (notice again the modernist urge to get round, or under, historical categories). In this case the imaginative corolary in Birtwistle's richly stocked inner world is the painting of Piero de la Francesca. In Piero's *Scourging of Christ*, we see the scourging happening in *this* corner, while over *there* three men discourse about something else; a peculiar disjunction mirrored exactly in the curious disjunctions of Birtwistle's music, where processes proceed in ignorance of each other, and yet in their separateness compose a mysterious unity.

Similar lists of creative preoccupations could be drawn up for any significant living composer. In one column, you would find the authors, paintings, landscapes, ideas that act as inspiration; in the second column, the musical devices that incarnate those ideas. The one column is as vital as the other; again (it's an important point) notice the profound contrast with Mozart, whose 'inner world' is an irrelevance – we don't need access to it to appreciate the music. For another example, as joyous as Birtwistle is melancholy, one could take the phenomenally gifted and prolific Danish composer Per Nørgård. Like Birtwistle's, his private mythology has the beginnings of a coherence; he's fascinated by the schizophrenic Swiss artist Wölfli, and by the apocalyptic visions of William Blake. One gets the sense of a composer for whom music reveals a secret order, something which at once underlies mundane appearances, and transcends them (this tension between an 'analytical', quasi-scientific approach to the truth behind appearances, and a transcendental one, is a common one in modernist creativity). We turn to the music, hoping this will bring order to a world only partially ordered. And what we find, in many pieces, is a vastly ambitious ordering system: the so-called 'infinity series', a pattern that as its name suggests is endlessly self-renewing, while retaining a degree of self-similarity. Even before we hear a note of the music that it generates, the infinity series has a seductive intellectual fascination. And in the sound of a piece like the Second Symphony, it does indeed create an intoxicating sense of a music that could generate its own substance for ever.

If it's true that in the music of these composers, and a handful of others, the conjunction of reinvented musical categories and an imagined world produces beautiful, suggestive, and power-fully moving works of art, then we have gone some way towards rescuing modern music from the charge of irrelevancy. But not all the way. A suspicion remains that what we're dealing with in each case is not a reinvented realm of music, but a private language. But as Wittgenstein has shown – to most people's satisfaction – a private language is an impossibility. It might be more accurate, if rather harsh, to describe these works as rhetorical tricks, in which a dubious private attempt at reshaping music's realm engages in a mutual-support pact with a mythology which, being private, must be equally dubious. But two privacies do not add up to something truly public, any more than a man can lift himself into the air by his own bootstraps.

To a degree, the best works by Birtwistle, Nørgård, Kurtág, and a handful of others are their own best defence against the charge. Works of art are not logical propositions, after all, and if these succeed in moving and inspiring a large number of people (which they do; the idea that these works appeal only to handful of groupies is a myth) then that is the surest sign that they do indeed belong to a truly public realm. But the sceptics will only be totally convinced if it could be shown that some modernist composers don't need a private mythology, or pretentious programme notes, to support their music.

This is a hard if not impossible condition to satisfy totally. There is no art composer working today, whether modernist or neo-Romantic, minimalist or maximalist, whose music does not require some degree of explication. The programme note, much as everyone professes a dislike for it, is even more inescapable now than it was for Berlioz and Bruckner. And something which requires a programme note must be so to speak tainted by the private. A truly public musical utterance, like a pop song (well, most pop songs) or a dance, or a march, needs no explication; its meaning is given by its use, or – if it is something designed to be listened to – expressed through signs that every member of the culture will understand. This is the ironic result of the cult of 'pure' music; it has led to a situation where nothing can be pure, where everything needs a new-fangled supporting context to make sense. This is just as true for a work with a traditional title, like 'Symphony', as it is for *Aporia 3*; because these days an old genre can only be invoked within 'scare quotes'.

However, there are degrees; some composers get closer to a self-explaining 'purity' than others. Take Elliott Carter, the grand old man of American modernism. His music is not bathed in some private world; he has his enthusiasms, certainly, but they don't colour the musical experience. As if in compensation for that, his music is rich in formal devices which, to some extent, have become public property. His ingenious method of negotiating a smooth passage between different tempi, known as 'metric modulation', has left its mark on at least two generations of composers beneath him, and his way of conjuring the entire material of a piece out of one or two germinating chords has also been massively influential. Part of the reason these techniques enjoy a wide currency (and not just among composers) is that they are extensions, or reworkings, of the traditional musical realm. One can find precedents for metric modulation as early as Monteverdi, and the idea of coaxing a whole piece from a few germinating ideas is nothing but good old-fashioned German organicism, of the sort that underlies a Brahms intermezzo – or a Sibelius symphony.

Another example of a new technique whose very name signals a connection with music's traditional realm is 'micropolyphony', a term conceived by the Hungarian composer György Ligeti. In the mid-1960s, while working on his Requiem, Ligeti found that his gropings towards a new sort of syntax were all prompted by the question: 'Can one find a way of working with intervals and even harmonies, which are innately obsolete materials, in a way different from before?' The answer was yes, but only when they had been passed through a technique that would denature them, scrub them clean of their usual meanings and functions. You hear that in an early piece like *Atmosphères* for orchestra, where out of a chromatic burbling haze, a chord made up of the black notes on a piano magically emerges, which casts a sudden innocent brightness over the music. Is this a change of colour, or a harmonic effect? The fact that we can't give an unequivocal answer is part of the point; ambiguity of perception is what Ligeti is after. 'Micropolyphony' is another ambiguous term. As the name suggests, it is a kind of musical texture made up of the play of individual lines, just like ordinary polyphony; what makes it 'micro' is the fact that the intervals between the notes making up the lines are tiny, the metre is fluid, and the lines themselves are tangled up with each other rather than separated out. Is the result a kind of texture that one perceives as a whole, or is it a discourse made up of separate elements? Again, the fact that the music at one moment guides towards one interpretation, and the next moment towards another, is the secret of its fascination.

The combination of an in-built ambiguity within the syntax, and the presence of subliminal connections with 'old music', go some way to making Carter's and Ligeti's music a genuine collective experience. A more radical approach to the problem of uniting the musical realm has been taken by Pierre Boulez. At the beginning of the twenty-first century it is more clear than ever that

Boulez is the conscience, as well as the mind, of contemporary music. More than any of his contemporaries, he is deeply troubled by the multiplicity of new music, and has laboured mightily to provide the means whereby modernist music could once again be a singular, unified realm of music. Boulez, underneath his radical appearance, is deeply conservative, even atavistic. His ideal of music is the marriage of action and symbol achieved in ritual; as he put it, music should be 'frenzy and collective spells'. This is why he insists, in his book *On Music Today*, that what really matters are 'global, generalisable solutions'. For him, useful techniques like 'micropolyphony' or 'metric modulation' aren't enough. He pours scorns on *ad hoc* 'recipes' that remain the 'personal property of their creators', and elaborates a musical world unified by the choice, at the outset of the creative process, of a single row of 'quantities' which when permutated would yield an entire piece.[2]

The advantage of Boulez's heroic enterprise (derided these days as 'Stalinist') was that it could – in theory at least – unify the shattered musical world at a stroke, at both the material and conceptual level. It provided a way of unifying higher-level things like melodies, harmonies, rhythms (though it could be said that it unified those things at the not inconsiderable cost of destroying them). But it also provided the answer to the question raised at the beginning of this chapter, of how the new multiplicity of sounds, created by new technologies (and by old technologies used in radical ways, above all the orchestra), could be made to yield a discourse.

Before you can elaborate a grammar, you have to work out the 'parts of speech'. The analogy between musical and verbal units can be drawn, but it's a shaky one. Music has its letters – notes – which can be combined to form words (phrases or motifs) which in turn combine to form bigger units (melodies). But there's no analogue in music for different verbal functions like verb, conjunction and noun. In any case the postwar avant-gardists – above all Boulez – shied away from the parallel, because it invoked the very categories – melodies, phrases – they wanted to abolish. They inclined more towards purely formal systems, more akin to bits of mathematics like set theory. Given a large, potentially infinite set of sounds, a way had to be found to order them. And given that there was nothing in the sounds which suggested a function – there were no verbs, no nouns – the best way seemed to treat them in the most neutral way possible, as mere quantities. A sound could be assigned a value, or rather a range of values – one for its pitch, one for its loudness, one for its 'colour'. If the sound consisted of an aggregate of simple sounds, its density could be given a value as well (so a chord consisting of seven 'notes' would have density 7).

When notes are turned into numbers in this way, they become abstract; their sensuous immediacy retreats into the background, and what is foregrounded are the numerical patterns they embody. But numbers can be manipulated in all kinds of ways which owe nothing to musical craft or tradition. If the intervals of a chord A can be spelled 2,5,3 and chord B as 2,3, then a composer of speculative disposition, and shaky grasp of musical reality, might conceive the idea of 'multiplying' chord A by chord B. Having multiplied the numbers, the results have to be converted back into notes; the question then was to what extent the notion of 'multiplying' had been given any musical sense. There are numerous ways of conceiving this 'multiplication', the most intelligent of which is described in Pierre Boulez's formidable attempt to create a new musical grammar in *On Music Today*. The results are really quite interesting, but in a way that has no connection whatever with what we understand by 'multiplication'. What one hears is chord A 'thickened' by being layered above a transposed version of itself. All Boulez has done is add a twist to that good old-fashioned element of music, transposition, a workaday bit of musical technique that Broadway MDs and orchestral players have to deal with every day. This is the secret of Boulez's massive authority: speculative intelligence, and traditional musicality at a stratospherically high level, are joined in a way no one else can match.

Where did it come from, this peculiar obsession with formalism and numbers? It was in part a symptom of that fervent faith in statistical methods which seemed to grip every discipline in the postwar decades. The avant-garde music of Nono, Boulez and Xenakis treats musical material the way 1950s sociologists like Talcott Parsons treated the human subject, as a mere statistical point, deprived of history, whose movements could be explained by mathematics. But it also had a more specifically musical forebear. The twelve-note method of Schoenberg, invented in the 1920s, combined a peculiar obsession with one number in particular – 12, the number of semitones in the chromatic scale – with an interest in intervals. In the absence of any key-centre there had to be a new source of identity, and it was provided by unique ordering of twelve notes invented for every piece composed according to the new method. That order was perceived as a shape – a series of up and down steps or leaps.

However abstract it might appear, Schoenberg's system was saved from spinning off into abstract speculation by its historical baggage. The most potent force in Schoenberg's Suite or Serenade is his determination to emulate Bach and Brahms, not his ingenuity with numerical patterns. No such baggage constrains Boulez's new-fangled world, which does indeed have the potential to proliferate into infinity, each pattern begetting a new one in a never-ending chain. Boulez's own music betrays this dizzying tendency to 'proliferation' as the composer calls it, tending always towards a maximum density of incident and detail. The composer acknowledges the staggering possibilities of his system, but doesn't think of them as problematic. 'Imagination must learn to master them', he says stonily.

The other curious, and ironic, feature of these systems is that, despite their universalist aspirations, their actual sound is very personal and localized. Boulez's striving towards 'global, generalisable solutions' leads, in the case of his own music, to something full of instantly recognizable gestures: held chords which issue suddenly in an explosive volley of notes, giant resonant sonorities which change colour as their component parts fade at different rates, serried ranks of violas trilling away in support of a florid, somewhat Eastern-sounding soprano line. You can almost lay it down as a rule that the more elaborate and ambitious the speculative aspect of a modernist composer's music, the more local, and full of personal fingerprints, its sound is likely to be. And this is by no means something to regret; on the contrary, these signs of humanity and personality are what make Boulez's music attractive, and even lovable.

This is true even of those composers whose 'systems' were created precisely to eradicate any trace of personality. The American composer John Cage hated the idea that music might be a vehicle for self-expression, and his creative life was a 60-year search for ways of releasing sounds from intention and expressivity in order to 'be themselves'. His early attempts used patterns of sound and silence derived from Indian rhythms. In *Sonatas and Interludes* for prepared piano those patterns are combined with another, totally separate technique, which Cage used to turn the piano into something richly strange. By placing bolts and rubber bands at precisely specified places within the piano's innards, he turned it into a percussion instrument which now and then recalls the Javanese gamelan, and at other times suddenly returns to a piano sound. The result, according to the composer, is a manifestation in Western terms of the ancient Indian system of emotional states, 'and their common tendency towards tranquillity'. But to the listener it is something else, a world of peculiar delicate charm and humour, whose piquant flavour – poised between East and West – is like nothing else in music. Later in his life, Cage went further in his search for 'non-intention', welcoming chance and chaos into his music.

But even at his most deliberately chaotic, Cage still sounds like Cage. If there's one thing his work proves it's that there really is no escape from personality. The result of his humorous, gently witty skirmishes with chance and nonsense were simply another private view of the world, to be set alongside those other private worlds of Ligeti, Boulez, *et al*. And like them it claimed the realm of music for itself.

Of course, none of these claims can be sustained, because all these worlds are to a degree mutually exclusive. What unity the new music world possesses is really an institutional one, in the sense that the specialist venues, festivals and radio programmes where audiences can hear Boulez are also the very same ones where they can hear Cage and Ligeti. The same goes for the sources of financial support for new music. If the Arts Council of England helps to fund a performance of a piece by John Cage, it's not because the official who made that decision actually shares Cage's anarchic/Zen Buddhist view of what music should be; it's an expression of the view that, in a pluralist society, Cage's view has a perfect right to exist. The same goes for Boulez, or neo-Romanticism, or minimalism. At the institutional level, the new music world is the projection, onto the expressive plane, of the pluralism of late-capitalist democracy. It's not animated by any real set of shared values; it's simply a neutral space where different aesthetics, different conceptions of what counts as music, can be displayed.

The contrast with, say, the Musikverein in Vienna *c*.1880, where music, architecture and social ritual are all expressions of a single world-view, seems absolute. However great the contrasts in aesthetic between the items on a concert pro-gramme – which could have embraced a wide historical purview, from Couperin to Mozart to Brahms – there was at that time a shared set of musical norms, a 'common practice', which united all the pieces. Over and above the stylistic differences, the pieces asserted the unity of music as a whole. That unity lent support to, and was supported by, the institutions of music which themselves were part of the cultural superstruc-ture of the governing class.

Compare that to the situation nowadays, which is doubly fragmented. A new music event does not share in, or express, the value system of an entire class; it is merely a 'niche market' which appeals to a tiny segment of the educated classes. And on the level of the musical material, each piece outlines its own world. These days, Bach, Thelonious Monk and John Cage could all be encountered within the space of single piano recital, or a Kronos Quartet concert.

To move between three such different worlds ought to be a profoundly shocking and disorien-tating experience. So shocking, in fact, that it should really be placed centre-stage as the fundamental category of experience in a new music concert, overriding any particular responses to particular pieces. Why then do we never hear anything about it? Why is the fundamental fact about a new music concert that it presents the listener with a set of incommensurable experiences never mentioned in books about new music?

The reason is that the authors of these books, just like the directors of music-funding policies, subscribe to the pluralist aesthetic ideology (or, perhaps it would be more accurate to say, they swim in it – and therefore don't notice it, as the fish never notices the sea it swims in). That ideology says that the effect of the pluralist viewpoint on musical experience is precisely nil. We can pass, without discomfort, from Glass to Boulez to Piazzolla precisely because the framework is neutral (or 'non-judgemental', to use the proper jargon term) with respect to all of the things within it.

There must be a danger, though, that the audiences who inhabit that neutral frame will come to share its neutrality. But when neutrality passes from artistic policy to a category of experience we have to give it a different name: indifference. The word 'neutral' has no meaning in aesthetics, which is value-laden in its essence.

Thus every new music concert – at least, every one containing modernist music – becomes a battleground. In front of us, on the platform, we are faced with something which demands our allegiance; something whose philosophy, technique, and sound will most likely be in stark opposition to the next piece, and the previous one. But around us, in the concert hall, in the very air we breathe, we receive a different message; one that says, 'don't worry; you don't really have to choose between these things; it's only music after all'. So there is a tension both between the works themselves, and between the works and the frame that seeks to contain and neutralize them. No wonder the faces at a new music concert tend to appear rather strained.

It is to fight the suffocating tolerance of the institution of new music that new music itself becomes so dogmatic and obstreperous (or used to; recently it's become appallingly good-mannered). Sometimes that fight is made at the level of the nose-thumbing gesture; sometimes it goes to the root of what music is. The very notion of 'the aesthetic object' has seemed to many to be suspect, given that it's so easily tamed. The attempts to rethink the aesthetic object, to refigure the relationship between idea, medium and audience, will be the subject of the next chapter.

NOTES

1. Tawaststjerna, E. (1986). *Sibelius*. Trans. Robert Layton, London, Faber & Faber, vol. 2, p. 76.

2. Boulez, P. (1971). *On Music Today*. Trans. Richard Rodney Bennett and Susan Bradshaw, London, Faber & Faber.

5

❧

Text, Body, Machines

The thing which mediates that relationship is of course the *text*, that defining feature of the Western tradition. Even now, the word 'composer' still evokes the image of someone at a desk, putting notes on paper, even though for many composers the image is a false one (because their music is made directly from sounds in the studio, rather than written down).

This clinging by many composers to the text is often glossed as a preference for live musicians over synthesized sound-sources. There's no necessary connection between these two things; a preference for the human element can just as easily be expressed through acoustic forms of improvisation, such as jazz, or forms of live music-making where the material is learnt 'by heart', like pop. Nonetheless composers of the old sort who write scores insist that one reason they compose the way they do is that they treasure the live element in music, the unpredictability that attends every new performance of their text in sound. And they say – with some justice – that in terms of sensuous and expressive force, no sampled voice or violin or tabla ever quite measures up to the real thing.

But there's a deeper reason why many musicians treasure text-based forms of musical creation. Writing a score is a proof that one possesses that mysterious thing, 'craft' (if the score is a competent one). There is a profound dichotomy between the 'craft' of music and the 'know-how' that goes with using technology. The distinction is partly institutional; 'craft' is taught in places like conservatoires, whereas 'know-how' is partly a matter of reading the manual, partly a matter of hanging around the places where the know-how can be picked up, like studios. (There are courses in music technology, but they sit uneasily in university and conservatoire syllabuses, precisely because they lack the element of craft.) The hostility between technology and craft is a long-standing one within art music. It became more heated in the nineteenth century as music's technology (i.e. the orchestra) became more elaborate. As Carl Dahlhaus points out, the expansion of music's technical means was a symptom of the impossibility, in the modern age, of expressing 'depth' in a simple, unselfconscious way:

In the first half of the [nineteenth] century profound and significant thought could legitimately be expressed in straightforward musical language, inasmuch as directness and simplicity were in accord with the romantic *Zeitgeist*. But in the second half of the century such a mode of expression at once came under suspicion of being kitsch (and since aesthetic cases are tried by public opinion, not by learned judges, suspicion is already tantamount to conviction). Therefore, if it was not to sink to basement level, musical neo-romanticism had to have recourse to complex compositional techniques (such as lie behind the apparently artless simplicity of *Die Meistersinger*), that is, to the 'industrial machinery' of a Berlioz that aroused Wagner to simultaneous admiration and denunciation. The 'machinery', in other words the deployment of musical technology (as opposed to musical craftsmanship, of which Wagner and Berlioz were considered not fully masters by some of their contemporaries, and not always those who were the worst judges), though it is in one respect a document of the spirit of the industrial, positivist age, is not so much a denial of the neo-romantic 'poetic intention' as an essential factor in its musical realisation. It is the artistic quality of the realisation which distinguishes it from kitsch, which cannot bridge the gulf between its primitive techniques and its 'poetic' pretensions.[1]

Notice how, in that last sentence, the idea of artistic quality is elided with the idea of technical sophistication, as if the latter were an infallible path to the former. That assumption is often made in modern music. In its anxiety to avoid kitsch, it flies into the opposite extreme of identifying complication with true complexity, and a fussy elaboration with subtlety. The best composers are aware of that danger, which is why one finds, in composers as diverse as Britten and Kurtág, a yearning for simplicity, side by side with the realization that complexity of means is unavoidable.

Simplicity and complexity are slippery words, because each can masquerade as the other. There comes a point when piled-up complexity collapses into a single, global perception; for example, if a polyphonic tangle becomes complicated enough the ear and brain give up the attempt to unravel them, perceiving instead a texture or colour (the interesting borderline between simplicity and complexity is a favourite territory for modern composers, particularly the Hungarian composer György Ligeti). And a complex thought-process can result in a sound of startling bareness; there are plenty of examples of this in new music, from Webern to Birtwistle. What one never finds in art music of the last half-century is the apparently artless simplicity of a Schubert or even of a Stravinsky (I say 'apparently' because Schubert's 'Grüne' or Stravinsky's piano duets for children are perfect examples of the art that conceals art).

What one can say for sure is that the avoidance of kitsch is really to do with the avoidance of habit, and stereotyped linkages between musical material and expressive qualities. This is why, in modern music, the business of keeping craft separate from know-how is even more vital than it was in Wagner's time. To do that, anything within craft that smacks of 'know-how' must be eliminated; which really means, eliminating anything that's to do with producing formulaic expressiveness. It's the element best summed up in composer Nigel Osborne's splendid phrase, 'junk professionalism'.[2] This is the version of craft possessed by every TV sound-track composer: the sort that knows how to create a gathering tension that lasts exactly 47 seconds, the sort that can summon up an image of Edwardian England in a few deft touches. One can summarize 'junk professionalism' as the ability to produce good pastiche, pastiche being really the same as kitsch, but without the latter's pretensions to being genuine art.

The craft that can fashion a perfect fugue is of a completely different sort, because there's no pre-set expressive aim. In modernist music, the purity of craft goes even further; it becomes a means of investigation as much as creation. This is most starkly revealed in 'classical' forms of electronic music. Here craft is nothing to do with the know-how of current forms of electronic music, which is a matter of knowing how to link up effects units, and how to run software. It's to do with understanding the nature of sound, and sound-synthesis, and how these can lead to a proper 'grammar' for music.

We see this determination to purge craft of know-how at its most heroic in Stockhausen. His approach to creating electronic music in the 1950s was rooted in the simple perception that, at bottom, the different parameters of music are in fact made of the same 'substance', namely periodic vibration. This means that any parameter can be converted into any other, just as mechanical energy can become heat, and vice versa. Take a rhythm made of regularly or irregularly spaced pulses, loop it so that it repeats, and speed it up by a factor of 30: you'll now hear a single pitch with a distinct colour or timbre. Take a sustained sound and slow it down progressively, and there comes a point where the sound resolves itself into its constituent pulses. Combine this with a mystic vision of music which sees it as the echo of cosmic rhythms and vibrations, and with a lingering attachment to Schoenberg's 'serial' principle – now broadened to embrace other aspects of music beyond pitches – and you have a music that promises to be rigorous in its portentousness.

To what extent that conceptual beauty 'communicates' through the sounds it makes is a fiercely contentious matter. Stockhausen is as great a showman as he is musical thinker, and he's not averse to using a rhetorical flourish to underline a conceptual idea in the most blatant way. The *locus classicus* is that admittedly striking moment in his 1961 masterpiece *Kontakte*, where we hear a noisy, siren-like pitch descend with a sound like a plunging propellor-plane into the depths, where it magically converts, before our very ears, into its constituent 'dots'. Like so many of the great moments in modern music, it forms a class by itself – you can't imitate it without falling into pastiche.

But even Stockhausen's dramatic flair can't always overcome the difficulties of electronic music. There's the narrow range of reference – spaceships and dystopian anxiety is about the limit of it. (Though the rival group of electronic music composers based at the Groupe de Recherche Musicale in Paris had the opposite problem. Being made from 'found' material, rather than newly synthesized sounds, their music's range of reference is altogether too wide, in fact 'referring' is all it's capable of. Beguiling though the sounds of a lonely night walk are in Pierre Schaeffer and Pierre Henry's *Symphonie pour un homme seul*, they hardly add up to any kind of musical discourse.)

But a deeper problem is that electronic music obliterates the distinction between conception and execution on which the whole notion of classical music has depended. That distinction depends on the separate existence of the conception, in the form of the text. But electronic music has no text in that sense. There is no 'score' of Stockhausen's electronic masterpiece of 1956, *Gesang der Jünglinge*, though there is a series of instructions which, if followed exactly, might allow you to reconstruct the sounds.

You might say: surely 'following a set of instructions to recreate the sounds' is precisely what a score allows us to do? But this misunderstands the way a score differs from a blueprint. A blueprint is a way of producing mechanically exact copies. It yields something whose nature can be predicted, and therefore guaranteed. But there are no guarantees when a score is realized. The performance may be lousy, or it may be brilliant; either way, it is not identical with the 'work', which hovers somewhere behind or above the score, as the limit point towards which all performances tend.

That gap between conception and realization has proved to be both fascinating and bothersome to composers. Fascinating, because it gives music a peculiar metaphysical duality: is the identity of a piece given in the the score I'm holding, or in the performance of the score I heard last night? It's also bothersome, because the aspect of music that's revealed in performance is clearly outside the composer's control. In the early period of the 'common-practice' in Classical music – i.e. from around 1600 to 1800 – composers were easygoing, more tolerant of the performer's freedom. The text had not yet become the fetishized object it has now become. The reason was that at that date the text was neither a blueprint, nor the incarnation of some Platonic conception of a piece, to be treated with reverence. It was more like a recipe for performance, which like any recipe can be tweaked in its ingredients and still yield the same dish as last time. When a performer in, say, a Rossini comic opera, or an early sixteenth-century madrigal exerted his or freedom to embellish the text, or to realize in a personal way the harmonic framework contained in the 'figured bass', the identity of the piece was not threatened. It was this flexibility which allowed for that social 'portability' mentioned in Chapter 1, whereby a sacred vocal piece could turn up in a rearranged form as lute piece, or a secular song, and still be recognizable as essentially the same piece. The social mobility of music was facilitated by the distinction, in each piece, between its 'accidents' – the particular sonorous dress in which it appeared in each of its social settings – and its essence, which was the abstract pitch-and-rhythm structure that subsisted beneath.

But as the classical 'realm' became established, this area of freedom was whittled away. Beginning in Germany in the late eighteenth century and spreading gradually to the rest of the classical music world (Italy, with its operatic tradition, held out the longest) the idea of a piece as a fixed 'work', whose notes were fixed for all time on the page, and to which any performance could only be an approximation, took root.

In contemporary music, the new inviolability of the text takes on a rather pathological aspect. There is a tendency, throughout the twentieth century, for musical scores to become crowded out with expressive markings, and a fussy elaboration of detail. Go to the new music section of any music library, and pick an orchestral score at random, and the chances are you'll be faced with a complicated array of symbols that makes a Beethoven symphony look simple. The increasing complication of texture and detail goes hand-in-hand with an ever-increasing specificity of instruction to the performer, often expressed verbally. The tendency reaches an almost comic hypertrophy on the last page of Ligeti's Cello Concerto, where there are more words than notes on the page.

The amusing thing about all this is that composers and performers still talk about their relationship in the same terms that Brahms and Liszt did a century and a half ago. Harrison Birtwistle wants his performers to feel free to interpret, and put their own personality into his music, while one of his most distinguished performers, the conductor Elgar Howarth, insists that his job is to be the composer's servant, realizing the dots and instructions as accurately as he can.

This is one of the clearest examples of how, in modern music, old ways of thinking and old aesthetics keep their fascination long after changing practices should have rendered them void. The apparent contradiction between Birtwistle's view and Howarth's view was, in the Romantic era, not a contradiction at all; it was a fruitful tension. But today it really *is* a contradiction, and not just because these scores specify every action so minutely that they seem more akin to blueprints. 'Musicality' and personality are these days harder to discern in performance because the area of 'free play' between score and audience – the area once occupied by things like a sense of style, or the knowledge of how to realize the summary outlines of a figured bass – has disappeared. It was in the dialogue with these inherited categories that performers could reveal themselves as quirky or restrained, tasteful or vulgar, inspired or routine. Without them, the markers of expressivity tend to shrink to the gestural, or the merely quantitative. A bigger *ritenuto* (slowing down), a more exaggerated attack, are read as being 'more expressive' – there are no opposing categories of idiom or style that might lead one to say 'actually no, that's overdone'.

This is the reason why modernist music lacks what one might call the 'social body'. The subtle lift of a waltz, the firm tread of a march – these are public categories of movement. But modern music has deprived itself of these (until around two decades ago, when the rhythms of disco, then of dance music, started to invade classical music). Its body language is purely personal, and becomes therefore the index of a purely personal inner life. What that gloomy cultural pessimist Adorno said about Schoenberg's *Erwartung* of 1910 – that it sounds like a body shrinking beneath a series of blows or shocks – can still be said of many composers now. The sudden violent eruptions in Birtwistle's *Secret Theatre*, the shriek and percussive thwack that rounds off Simon Holt's *Capriccio Spettrale*, the *fortissimo* ambushes of Olga Neuwirth's *Vampyrotheone* – all these impinge directly on the nerves, with no intervening idiom to soften the shock. In fact you could put that statement the other way round, and say that these moments are a faithful transcription, into sound, of what it feels to like to be traumatized.

Nobody likes to be traumatized, of course, which explains the failure of this kind of music to reach a mass market. But it could be asked why *any* listener not afflicted with masochism should want to seek out such music. A remark of Adorno might give us a clue. On the subject of modernism's unpopularity he said that 'the dissonances which horrify them [i.e. audiences] testify to their own conditions [i.e. as alienated from themselves]; for that reason alone do they find them unbearable'.[3] Stripped of its pessimism, that statement points us to a reason why this kind of music does have a genuine public, and why modernist music continues to resonate despite the strident announcements by its enemies that 'old new music is dead'. The shocks are a necessary ingredient of any idiom which honestly addresses our sensibility – which, for the Western urban sophisticates who make up new music's public, is essentially private, uninformed by public or social forms. They are, so to speak, one side of the coin of a music which is essentially lonely. The other side is a kind of beauty which is really the expression of a heightened, neurasthenically intense state of awareness. A literary analogue for these hallucinatory states would be those wonderful descriptions in Baudelaire of what it feels like to witness the dawn in a silent deserted city street after a sleepness night.

But many composers are in revolt against the fetishism of the text, and have tried to reinstate the more healthy, collaborative relationship that once existed between composer and performer. Again, it fell to Boulez to articulate an uncomfortable truth, which is that rethinking the relationship between text and performer isn't a matter of personal choice; it's something imposed on any composer who wants to be true to the times he finds himself in. For Boulez, the essence of the composer's task today is finding a balance between discipline and freedom; and to do that, he developed in the 1960s a way of loosening the text's hold on performers, while hanging on tightly to his role as 'author' of the text. His Third Piano Sonata includes a movement where bits of music are scattered across two large pages, rather than joined up in an unalterable progression. The pianist darts from one fragment to another according to which one takes his or her fancy, within certain rules. The composer compares the piece to a road-map of the city, which allows the reader to mentally traverse the city in a myriad different ways.

This is one of the most celebrated examples of so-called 'mobile' forms, for which there was a vogue in the 1950s and 1960s. What's curious about Boulez's piece is the way the freedom is tightly confined to the ordering of the fragments, which in themselves have exactly the same fastidiously notated detail as Boulez's 'normal' pieces. The same determination not to let go of the material of the piece can be seen in Preludes and Fugues for Strings by the Polish composer Lutosławski, where from time to time individual players are released from the conductor's beat. The freedom is only temporal; the notes are given by the composer, but their rhythm is created 'on the spot' by the performer. The combination of each person's freedoms leads to a different result at each performance, but Lutosławski is not really interested in what chance can give him. On the contrary, he takes infinite pains with these 'free' passages, adjusting the degree of freedom he offers the players until he's satisfied that all possible results will sound the way he wants them to. It's an odd sort of freedom that can only lead to what the composer wants to hear, and the truth is these pieces don't really change the paradigm of the 'text' as it's been conceived in classical music for most of its history.

This is why these attempts to subvert the text end up sounding remarkably like the fully written-out scores by the same composer. I would defy anyone not already familiar with the piece to discern which movement of Boulez's Third Sonata is 'strict' and which 'free'. But though the granting of this sort of performer freedom may not be readily discernible in this idiom, there is another sort whose effects are more apparent to the listener. During the 1950s and 1960s there was a vogue for graphic forms, where instead of writing notes the composer would indicate by graphic means the kind of sound he was in search of: a thick wedge across the stave to indicate a cluster-chord, a snowstorm of random dots to depict a texture made up of short sounds, like raindrops on a roof. Here the decisions as to which notes to play at which moment are left up to the performer; 'accuracy' consists in finding the right aural correlative for those curious squiggles and whirls on the page.

By the 1970s both kinds of freedom were on the wane. It was a sign that within the very idea of notated music there is an irresistible pull towards the traditional model of one symbol per note. Among the many composers who trod the road back to conventional notation was the American experimental composer Morton Feldman. Many of his early scores from the 1950s use a form of graphic notation, where pitch and duration are only sketchily indicated. But from the 1970s onwards his pieces are fully notated. The difference in sound-world is instantly perceptible; the later pieces, while just as withdrawn, muffled and utterly static as the earlier ones, are more precisely imagined. One hears *pianissimo* chords, rather than *pianissimo* clusters of pitches. But without looking at the score no one would ascribe the change to a granting (in the 1950s) of freedoms to the performer, and then their withdrawal in the 1970s. This is because from the listener's point of view, there's nothing to distinguish which aspect of a sound belongs to a performer, and which to the composer. The inherited 'performer' idioms that allow us to draw that distinction have vanished.

The truth is that the whole notion of the mobile form is an incoherent one, which is why most of the composers that at one time employed it – Feldman, Lutosławski, Birtwistle, Boulez – eventually abandoned it. This is true even of those composers whose concept was much more extreme, like Earle Browne. His *25 Pages* consists, unsurprisingly, of 25 pages of music, on which pitches and relative durations are indicated but not the tempo. The pages can be played by one pianist, or distributed among 25 pianists, or any number in between. The kinship with Boulez's road-map idea is just about discernible, though Browne himself prefers the analogy of an Alexander Calder 'mobile'. On the face of it, the score here recovers the role it had in seventeenth-century Italy, namely as a 'recipe' for performance.

But in the works of John Cage we see something more radical still, which is the dissolving away of the concept of the 'work'. A mobile is after all still one *thing*, which can be viewed from infinitely many perspectives. But in John Cage's *Variations III* there is no object which the score produces; instead a series of instructions is specified by tossing a set of transparencies bearing black circles onto a sheet of white paper. Out of the myriad superimposed circles thus produced, the performer (or performers) choose one group of interlocked circles, which serves as the score; these describe a set of actions with a certain number of variables. The actions need have nothing to do with sound; they could consist of gestures, or actions involving props.

This piece was the high-water mark of Cage's step-by-step annihilation of 'music' as we know it.

His aim was to use a 'score' to subvert intention, rather than reveal it. He wanted to drain away the psychological tension that was such a feature of Western music, the 'bullying' dynamism he so abhorred in Beethoven, in order to let sounds and actions 'be themselves', that is, savoured for their own qualities rather than as part of an ordered structure. To achieve that he had to burst out from the neutral aesthetic frame of the concert I mentioned in the last chapter. His earlier work can be contained – just – within that frame. Cage's *Dream* for piano could sit quite comfortably alongside music by Satie and Debussy in a piano recital. But *Variations III* is so extreme in its projection of an alternative world-view that it can allow of no competitors. It commandeers the entirety of the space in which it occurs; no other world-view can be projected alongside it, least of all the aesthetic one projected by conventional 'pieces of music'.

One might consider this no less 'bullying' than Beethoven. Or one might consider the performing of a set of inscrutable actions with a perfectly straight face not as a mystical 'letting go' of will and intention, but as a gateway to stupefying boredom. Fine, Cage would say; as the mystics teach us, boredom can lead to enlightenment. Or one might just laugh out loud. That's also fine by Cage; if the photographs of him are anything to go by, he spent much of his life laughing (laughter is an aspect of Cage's work that most of his commentators pass by, though whether because they're embarrassed by it or too solemn to notice it is a moot point).

So in one respect Cage's most radical work is actually deeply traditional; it is based on the premise that any public event must project a unified world-view. In achieving that, Cage also points towards a solution of the old problem mentioned in Chapter 1: how to make the content of an 'occasion without an occasion' (that is, the traditional concert) seem anything other than arbitrary. Cage's solution is to make music merge with life, by having his pieces assume exactly the haphazard quality that real life has. Ideally, therefore, his pieces should be coterminous with life and infinitely long. He couldn't achieve that, but he never lost his feeling that the limited time-frame of a public event was inimical to his project.[4]

Cage's is a drastic solution to the problem of modern music's multiplicity, and the truth is it only works because we know it's just 'play'. Out there, beyond the concert hall where Cage's Zen view of the world has its protected space (Cage's work is like some hothouse bird that needs very special conditions to survive) there is the familiar world of technocratic rationality, to which we must all return. And because we live in that world, and not in a Zen monastery, we – and composers – fall back, time and again, to a mode of music-making that reflects the sensibility that that world produces: solitary, subjective, uninformed by public modes of address. It's a situation to be regretted, but Cage's work isn't a solution to it; though it can provide a beguiling, short-lived holiday.

Less drastic than Cage, though no less radical in intent, are the attempts by some composers to rethink the social setting of music (and the social dynamic *within* music) in a way that might actually have a bearing on the way we live now. One way of doing that seems, on the face of it, to be not really social at all. This is the re-emergence, within recent modernist music, of the body as a determining presence. The *body*, note, not the exacerbated lonely subjectivity that so much modernist music appeals to. The body, like society, has an objective existence. One way of revealing that existence is to push the body up against its limits. Brian Ferneyhough's music makes us forcibly aware of human limits, but in his case it's the impossibility of realizing the blizzard of instructions contained in his scores, which are surely the *ne plus ultra* of complication in music. A piece like *Unity Capsule* for solo flute squeezes as much information into a solo part as one normally finds in an orchestral score; the difference is it has to be realized by one person. The chances that any merely human performer could realize with total accuracy the piled-up layers of notation (some for rhythm, some for pitch, others for variety of timbre) are precisely zero. But according to the composer that doesn't matter; what counts is the struggle to achieve that accuracy. A good deal of so-called 'New Complexity' music from the 1980s and 1990s forces the performer along this *via dolorosa* of struggle and inevitable failure, and it's hard not to suspect that the extra *frisson* of intensity possessed by these pieces isn't due to their latent sadism.

A more sympathetic approach to objectifying the body in music is taken by the Italian composer Salvatore Sciarrino. The focus, though, is as much on the physicality of sound as of the body that makes it. In his exquisitely quiet and gentle chamber pieces, we hear right down into what Roland Barthes called the 'grain' of sound. This might seem reminiscent of Stockhausen's search for the basic 'atoms' of sound, but really it could hardly be more different. Whereas Stockhausen's music seems to be driven by a vehement dislike of the body and bodily rhythms, Sciarrino's basic categories are all bodily or material gestures. In Sciarrino's numerous pieces for solo flute, we're made aware of all the sounds normally forbidden by correct flute-playing: the sound of keys striking metal, the sound of breath through the tube. But most of all we're aware of music as an emanation of human breathing, an idea that fascinates Sciarrino. His orchestral piece *Un'Immagine di*

Arpocrate is governed by a vast breathing rhythm, each exhalation separated from the next by a cavernous silence.

The immense tranquillity of this music springs from its rootedness in a bodily action that is purely unconscious. And it's the unconscious aspect of the chosen bodily category that allows Sciarrino to treat the body as an ahistorical, asocial category. Cultural history bears him out; one can have histories of eating and sex, but not breathing. Ferneyhough's practice, of pushing the human organism up against its limits, might seem to be at the opposite pole to Sciarrino. But in fact it has exactly the same effect, of severing the body from its social reality. This is why these composers symptomatize so vividly something common to much new music, which is a curious absence of the erotic. The erotic is a key category of experience in Western art music. Tonality is regularly described in terms of arousal and expectation, tension and relief, and intertwined with this syntactic 'erotics' is a whole vocabulary of conventionalized expressions of desire and allure, masculinity and femininity. In music, as in life, desire tends to flout the rules of propriety, so the cultural theorists who see music as essentially 'transgressive' look at the way expressions of desire get the better of the music's grammatical rules, and of the composer's overt expressive intention. They've found a happy hunting ground for this form of transgression in

Western music from Monteverdi to Wagner,
which is one reason classical music has recently
acquired a new *chic* among cultural theorists. But
on the subject of new music they're silent. To take
one notable example, there is hardly a mention
of a living composer in Edward Said's *Musical
Elaborations*.[5]

Actually if these writers listened a bit harder
to new music (or even listened at all) they might
find that it too can be transgressive, subverting its
own logic, making links between categories that
once appeared watertight. Take the attempt by
Luciano Berio to marry collective, folk idioms
with modern practices, an attempt which has
necessarily involved idioms that invoke the 'social
body'. Compared to Sciarrino's hermetic purity,
Berio's music is 'dirty', full of cultural baggage; which is why his music is also so much
'thicker', so much richer in layers of meaning,
than Sciarrino's. Berio's mid-1970s masterpiece
Coro is an attempt to realize what he called a
'Utopian dream, which I know cannot be real-
ised. ... I would like to create a unity between
folk music ... and our music a real, perceptible,
understandable continuity between ancient popular music-making which is equally close to our
daily work and to our music'.[6] The piece is a
concatenation of many folk traditions round the
world, expressed through an exuberant polyphony of 40 solo voices, each paired with an

orchestral instrument. At times we might hear a duet between one of these pairs, that evokes one particular folk music; at other times all these separate experiences and cultures are subsumed in a tumultuous collective shout.

One of the reason Berio's music has a power to move is that it invokes those old collective idioms that once made us move to music. But what about the other side of the coin – the freedom of the performer to improvise within a given framework that has always been an essential element of traditional forms like folk song? Here Berio runs up against the dilemma of modernist music, which is that it can only hang on to the thing it values most – structural integrity – by 'composing' the musician's freedom. Because if the musician were given a genuine idiomatic freedom, the integrity of the artwork would be ruptured. There's no way a genuine Corsican folk singer could be woven into the vast tapestry of Berio's *Coro*. The folk tunes in that piece are all written out, complete with their spontaneous 'folky' inflections, to be performed by fully trained professionals. Style is absorbed into structure, and therefore kept in the composer's domain.

It's hardly surprising that the old text-based mind-set should persist, given that, even now, so much new music shares its venues, its performers, even its funding apparatus, with 'old' classical music. It's because the institutional framework of

classical music imposes its own aesthetic frame
that many composers and performers have tried
to escape it. This is why there's been, in the last
20 years, such an explosion of new performing
ensembles, dedicated to reconfiguring the relationship between text, performance and audience.
A group like the Steve Reich Ensemble repudiates
both the sound of the orchestra (there are no
strings, and lots of percussion), and its social
dynamics (there's no conductor). Some are even
more thorough-going in their detachment from
'normal' musical circles. For De Volharding,
the Amsterdam-based performing group created
by composer Louis Andriessen, the sound of the
ensemble, its aesthetic stance, its choice of venue
and repertoire, are all interlinked. The ensemble is
made up of loud instruments because it plays out
of doors. It plays out of doors because it wants to
reach a new audience, free from the bourgeois
rituals of the concert hall (Andriessen is a notable
soixante-huitard). And the music – particularly
that composed by Andriessen himself – gets its
stark, 'objective' intensity from the way the musical material is democratized; all the parts participate in the foreground, with nothing retiring
gracefully into the background as accompaniment.

Even so, one hierarchy is left in place: the
composer is still in charge of the proceedings,
exerting control via a score. Some groups have
gone through that final frontier, abandoning both

the governing text and the idea of a governing individual. What this leads to is group improvisation. Of course, being free from a score doesn't mean freedom *tout court*. There may be a governing idiom, as in jazz improvisation, or North Indian classical music. In classical music there is one, very minor sphere of activity where you encounter improvising within an idiom. This is in 'period performance', where some performers have mastered precisely those forms of 'musicality' that flourished before interpretation came along, such as realizing a figured bass, or decorating a melodic line in a Baroque aria. There are even pianists, like Malcolm Bilson, who can spontaneously improvise a cadenza to a Mozart piano concerto. More impressive – because it's a genuinely living tradition, rather than something revived – is the astonishing ability of French organists like Olivier Latry to improvise an entire symphony.

Less impressive as technical feats, but more symptomatic of the modern temper, are those strange and unsettling forms of improvisation undertaken by groups like AMM, the Sonic Arts Union and MEV (Musica Elettronica Viva). What makes them unsettling is the complete lack of any governing idiom. The whole effort of the players in these groups goes towards eliminating any trace of memory or habit from the sounds they make. What they're aiming for is the joy that comes from weightlessness, from liberating the moment, so that action and desire are united in an endlessly prolonged present. It's an aim as much mystical as musical, and it could be said that the banishing of the inherited vocabulary of music is a way of 'mortifying the flesh', a kind of stripping bare, very similar to the sort mystics have to go through. The instruments too must be mortified, by being played in strange ways that 'denature' them; better still, instruments are bypassed altogether by using new technology. Alvin Curran, a founder-member of the group MEV described how its members found themselves 'busily soldering cables, contact mikes, and talking about "circuitry" as if it were a new religion. By amplifying the sounds of glass, wood, metal, air and fire, we were convinced that we had tapped into the sources of the natural musics of everything ...'[7]

That approach leads to one type of free improvisatory music, the sort one could describe as contemplative. The other sort, which one could call ecstatic, is much more rooted in the body and in normal modes of playing, and is therefore hostile to technology. The radical left-wing composer/pianist Frederic Rzewski is a rare example of someone who started to make 'contemplative' improvisatory music, and realized he was on the wrong track. Having started out in the mid-1960s using technology, he rejected it, saying that he was 'becoming aware of the need for rediscovering our bodies', in order to make a music that was 'simple, physical, universal and liberating'.[8] The pianist Cecil Taylor, who came out of a jazz tradition (jazz has been just as prolific of 'free' improvisers as classical music) always knew technology wasn't for him, because 'it divorces itself from human energy, it substitutes another kind of force as the determinant agency for its continuance'.[9]

What these disputes show is that the attempt to escape from the text doesn't lead to some happy, conflict-free Utopia of instant fulfilment. The brave new world turns out to be full of contradictions and tensions, unnoticed in the first flush of discovery and exploration. Is improvisation really free, or is it bound to be compromised by habitual ways of playing and thinking, as both Cage and Boulez insisted? Does technology liberate the musical impulse, or does it merely stifle the physicality that ought to be part of music-making? Isn't the idea of using intention to subvert intention, as Cage did, a hopelessly self-contradictory notion? The experimental tradition was born out of a desire to make modern music simple; what it's actually done is to create a whole new set of puzzles, no less intractable, and endlessly renewable, than the age-old puzzles of the 'text' that it hoped to banish.

NOTES

1. Dahlhaus, C. (1980). *Between Romanticism and Modernism*. Trans. Mary Whittall, Berkeley, CA, University of California Press, pp. 13, 14.
2. Personal communication to the author.
3. Adorno, T. W. (1973). *Philosophy of New Music*. Trans. Anne G. Mitchell and Wesley V. Bloumster, London, Sheed & Ward, p. 9.
4. In the *Radio Happening II*, jointly given by Cage and Morton Feldman, Cage says: 'There is a resistance in me to have a new idea *for* an occasion. If I have a new idea I would like it to be somehow free of occasion.' (Quoted in Pritchett, J. (1993). *The Music of John Cage*. Cambridge, CUP, p. 144.)
5. Said, E. (1993). *Musical Elaborations*. New York, Columbia University Press.
6. Berio, L. (1985). *Two Interviews*. London, Marion Boyars, p. 148.
7. Young, R. (ed.) (2000). *Undercurrents: The Hidden Wiring of Modern Music*. London, Continuum, p. 244.
8. *Ibid.*, p. 43.
9. *Ibid.*, p. 245.

6

❧

Authenticities

What strikes one about these disputes between improvisers and chance composers, new complexity and experimentalism, is how very far away and very long ago it all seems. And yet all those kinds of music-making, and the personalities, are still very much with us. Rzewski is still composing (though he now writes his pieces out in the old-fashioned way), there are still free improvisers, New Complexity music is still being written (though it no longer seems very new). And there are still experimental composers out there, still giving concerts in underpopulated, draughty halls.

What is it that makes these things, all so different, share a sense of belonging to the past, of being not authentically of the 'new century'? It comes, surely, from the fervour of the disputes, the passionate taking of sides, something which seems to have fled the music world today. At bottom, these composers wanted to rediscover, or reinvent, the old unity, the one possessed by the common practice (though without its suffocating 'bourgeois' trappings). So important was that aim that no compromise was possible – which is why, in its effort to recreate a unity, modern music merely created its own multiplicity from within.

Unity, to a degree, entailed purity; which meant either keeping out other musics or refashioning them for the art music realm. But the striking thing about art music today is that its effort to keep itself distinct has finally relaxed. This has been simply a bowing to the inevitable; too many forces have been tending the other way, towards expansion and disintegration.

So what we find is that over the last 30 years or so, art music has itself taken on the vast plurality of music in the world at large. The expansion has partly been geographical. Contemporary art music was until recently located in Europe and America, with an outpost in Japan, a few pockets of activity in Latin America and a *samizdat* new music scene in the Soviet Union and Eastern Europe. Now 'new music' is everywhere. When the Soviet Empire came to its end, there was a great upsurge of interest in composers we'd barely heard of: Russians like Ustvolskaya, Denisov, and Schnittke, composers from other Soviet Republics (Arvo Pärt in Estonia, Giya Kancheli in Georgia) and Eastern European composers, most notably Henryk Górecki. A few years later it was China's turn. Suddenly we were hearing pieces by Tan Dun and Bright Sheng (the fact that the Chinese 'New Wave' composers chose to move to the West, like many of the Russians and Eastern Europeans, surely helped their music to be more widely known). And as soon as it was revealed, their music was distributed round the globe, joining the great roaring tide of music of all kinds that now assails every composer, and every listener, wherever they happen to live. The spectacle of the American Kronos Quartet playing music by black South African composers in Berlin is typical of the new music's new global presence.

Along with the geographical spread of new music – hugely abetted by the cheapness of digital recording techniques – has gone a bewildering multiplication of styles and means. Art music has a whole new cross-cultural face unimaginable a few decades ago. It has become open to the world, it takes what it wants from any source, East or West, high or low. The old class distinctions have disappeared. The pioneer cross-cultural composer Lou Harrison used to insist that art music could only borrow from another courtly or classical source. 'It will not do to mix Beethoven with blue-grass', he declared. Younger composers on the whole don't agree. John Adams mixes cartoon music and Schoenberg in his Chamber Symphony, Michael Dougherty celebrates American popular culture in concert works for symphony orchestra.

MUSIC: HEALING THE RIFT

The disappearance of the old hierarchies is well illustrated by the new music scene in Australia. 40 years ago Australian new music was an offshoot of European, particularly English music. Musical ties were dictated by old historical ones. In the 1970s, young Australian composers turned more to the musical cultures on their doorstep: Java, China, Japan, and to aboriginal sources. This was partly a gesture of repudiation of the colonial past. But that has now relaxed (relaxation, as will become clear, is a keynote of new music). These days Australian composers are just like composers everywhere, they take from every source equally, Britain included. Interestingly, the stylistic ties of Brett Dean, a composer only just into his 30s, are more Old World; his *Gesualdo* is a brilliant reworking of madrigals by the sixteenth-century Italian composer Carlo Gesualdo. But this isn't a sign of a reversion to old roots. The motivation is purely personal.

When a musical practice becomes this various, it becomes harder to discern or invent a narrative that makes sense of it all. 30 years ago new music was commonly described through the old 'great men' paradigm. Musical development was driven by a small number of seminal masterpieces, made, naturally enough, by men. These days the personalities seem smaller, and their doings no longer seem to be the determining factor in the changes sweeping across music. One looks elsewhere for causative factors, to vast impersonal forces: the advance of digital technology, the spread of recording, the *embourgeoisissement* of vast numbers of people in the developing world, which has brought in its wake the very same aspirational desire for classical music that the West had a century and a half ago. One sees this new sort of causative factor at work in the upsurge, since the 1980s, of women composers. Before this happened much new music was 'music for the boys', obsessed with systems, numbers, and gizmos. Some areas of new music still have that aspect, and they're still a male preserve (there are no women 'new complexity' composers). But taken as a whole, new music has become much more hospitable to women. The organizers of the various festivals, publishers and ensembles founded to give women composers a platform claim this as a success. But a much more likely factor is the softening of classical music's purity, the fading of the masculinist urge to systematize and make anew. And when one looks for the causal factor in *that* change, one finds no dominant figures setting the agenda, the way Boulez and a few others set the serial agenda. Nor could there be, because – to return to where we started – there are no agendas, there is no narrative.

It's tempting to say that the only unity among all these different practices is an institutional one. The thing that links Schoenberg, Ferneyhough,

Tan Dun and Michael Dougherty is that their music is played by the same orchestras and pianists, funded by the same Foundations and Cultural Ministries and private patrons, and heard in the same venues and on the same radio stations. But that only defers the question. The institutional support is surely a sign that there is, in our culture, a widely shared sense that certain sorts of music deserve nurturing and protecting, because they embody a particular set of values. The difficulty is to articulate those factors, in a practice that refuses to be read as a coherent whole.

But perhaps that's too hasty. Perhaps, beneath the appearance of sheer multiplicity, there is a direction and a narrative within art music in the new century. It seems to me that a new way of conceiving the art music realm has indeed been emerging, showing itself in a slow and all-embracing transformation, like the change of a season. We can get a clue to that conception as much from current discourse about music as from music itself. Take the use of the word 'symphonic'. At one time this had a precisely defined meaning. It was a piece for a particular medium, in a particular form, that took place in certain well-defined kind of public space. And it had a particular expressive weight; the symphony could express many kinds of mood, but overriding the mood of any given moment was a sense of important public address. The symphony was *the* medium of serious music.

What does 'symphonic' mean these days? Looking at the music press, PR announcements, award ceremonies for CDs, the answer seems to be – anything played by an orchestra. So a film score is just as symphonic as a Beethoven symphony. But look closer and you see that the term is being stretched even beyond this. The sampled factory and machine sounds of Anne Gosfield, a New York-based musician, were described by *Village Voice* as 'all electric, all noisy, but all *symphonic* and done by one of downtown's suavest musical thinkers'[1] (my italics). What on earth could the word 'symphonic' mean in that sentence? In terms of its media, its materials, its form, its social setting, Gosfield's music would seem to be anything but symphonic. In the end, one's driven to the conclusion that the term, if it has any content at all, is aspirational. The music aims for depth, it wants to be weighty. But this points to the problem with contemporary art music, a problem it shares with contemporary visual art. These days, the mere act of making a claim to seriousness seems, in some magical way, to be self-confirming. How do you substantiate such a claim? What distinguishes the deep in music from the merely obscure, the mysteriousness of a genuine artwork from the mystification of the fake one?

At one time, modern music had an answer to that question. Art was what the alliance of craft and tradition produced. These two things issued in works of music whose formal values gave substance and legitimacy to the meanings they expressed; craft rescued meaning from mere habit or cliché. Or, to put it the other way round, the inherited meanings were what saved the formal aspect of the music from falling into sterile intellectualism.

What has happened today is that the criteria, the markers of 'art music', have shifted from the outer to the inner. It's no longer the ingenious system, the vaulting ambition to reframe music's material, that binds classical music together. These days it's more an attitude, a certain stance to the act of making music which can express itself through many – some would say *any* – style, or vocabulary, or set of music/cultural norms. That attitude may well involve a refashioning of its chosen 'material', but isn't motivated by it. It goes under many names, but one will do here: 'authenticity'.

Authenticity is what everybody looks for in music. We want 'the real thing' as the Coca-Cola advert says, not a cheap imitation (or even an expensive one – in fact the expensive fake, when discovered, hurts more than the obvious fake, whose kitschy quality one can enjoy). But 'real-ness' shows itself in different ways. The question is whether each of those different ways matches up with its own musical practice, or whether the different conceptions of authenticity cut across different practices, creating their own map of the musical world. If it's the former, then modern music's authenticity will turn out to be nothing more than a redescription of its objective, technical features in more picturesque language. So we could discard it, as it would have no explanatory value. But if it's the latter, then 'authenticity' won't be riding piggy-back on anything else; it will have a real explanatory, or at least interpretative, force. So, armed with this distinction, we need to take another look at art music today, and ask: what kinds of value, what kinds of meaning do people find in it? Are they distinct from the meanings and values people find in jazz, or pop, or film music? And to what extent are those values correlated with a unique set of practices?

To get anywhere near an answer to those large questions we have to roam beyond art music, to see how value is described and asserted outside the art realm. And by value I mean that claim to a transcendental value which was once made only by art music, but is now made by every musical practice. Its basic paradigm is precisely the one elaborated by the art music realm in the last century: it divides the musical practice, whatever it is, into the deep and the shallow, the original and the cliché-ridden, the genuine and the commercial.

Music that can be described by the left-hand term in each pair is 'authentic'.

But those terms hardly describe the same qualities, however often they're elided in arts-speak. As you move across different musical categories, 'authenticity' takes on different meanings, often replete with the very same tensions that the ascriptions of value have in art music. Take world music, where the search for authenticity is most insistent. The Romantic idea that music might be apprehensible at some deep, visceral level, needing no knowledge of style or culture, lies at the root of the world music explosion. It's why a notable world music producer like Rob Gold can claim that knowledge actually gets in the way, because, after all, music is a 'universal language'. At the same time, world music wants its products to have the same kind of accreditation that dry-goods have. It uses the findings of ethnomusicology to give listeners that sense of authenticity that comes from careful research.

The co-opting of ethnomusicology by world music has been startlingly quick; but it's a dubious ally, as many of its practitioners regard world music with suspicion. And no wonder, because their careful, self-conscious descriptions (ethnomusicology is racked by the same methodological hang-ups and post-colonial guilt as all ethnographic disciplines) sit uneasily with the breezily confident tone of world music writing. The determination of world music writing to have it both ways – to explain and situate, and to insist that no explanation is needed – can be seen on the liner notes to the recent Songlines world music compilation. Here the lyrics of the Senegalese singer El Hadj N'Diaye are described as using 'proverbs and metaphors of everyday Senegalese speech to create poetic messages which convey great dignity, even if you don't understand a word of his native Wolof tongue'.[2] It's interesting that the author of this text acknowledges, in a back-handed sort of way, that not knowing Senegalese might be a problem when listening to a Senegalese song. What he doesn't say is that not knowing the language of Senegalese *music* might also be a problem. That presumably is because he doesn't feel music is a language that has to be learnt – it offers the direct, unmediated route to 'dignity' that the impenetrable words cannot.

In world music the tension is between particularism (music can only be understood in terms of the culture it expresses) and universalism (music as the common tongue of humanity). In other areas of music-making the fault-line in 'authenticity' runs in a different direction. This difference is partly to do with the gulf, in world music, between the cultural condition of the performers and receivers of the music, who by definition must be in the West. The performers are, in many cases, in serene possession of the musical culture, and take pride in an ancient lineage which is as much mythical as historical. The Uyghur musician Riyazdin Barat told me that his musical tradition goes back five thousand years, which makes it older than Mesopotamian civilization. In the West, makers and receivers are on the same side of a historical rupture, a moment when the tradition became aware that its own roots are distant, and to a degree unreachable. You even find historical awareness in pop, which can now boast half a century of history – easily long enough to allow for revivalisms to take place.

Jazz was nowhere near that old when the first Dixieland revival took place, in the late 1930s. That was the moment when jazz developed a language of authenticity, a language which has two aspects. It's the restless pushing out of boundaries – jazz as the 'sound of surprise' – but it's also a cleaving to some mysterious jazz 'essence', an essence which is itself torn between a performative definition (that mysterious 'swing') and historical ones (jazz as what the 'greats' did from King Oliver to Coltrane). You can feel the tension between them in the 'statement of intent' issued by Blue Note Records:

> Blue Note records are designed simply to serve the uncompromising expression of hot jazz and swing, in general. Any particular style of playing which represents an authentic way of musical feeling is genuine expression.

By virtue of its significance in place, time and circumstance, it possesses its own tradition, artistic standards and audience that keep it alive. Hot jazz, therefore, is expression and communication, a musical and social manifestation, and Blue Note Records are concerned with identifying its impulse, not its sensational and commercial adornments.[3]

Turning to classical music, there are different kinds of 'authenticity' in operation, according to where one looks. But each of them is riven with a similar ambiguity to the ones we've already encountered. In the standard repertoire of classical music, there is a sense – fading, but still lingering – that authenticity comes from being the heir to an unbroken tradition. This is part of the mystique of the silver-haired maestro. There are other aspects of that mystique of course – notably power and sex appeal – but being able to lay claim to a lineage lends a nimbus to conductors like Wolfgang Sawallisch, or pianists like Ivan Moravec, which isn't so different to the aura around a Malian *griot* like Cheik Amadou.

But there's another source of authenticity, which lays claim to the same authority, in the same repertoire, in the same spaces. This is the knowledge of tradition 'from the outside'. Starting as long ago as the late eighteenth century, but accelerating hugely in the nineteenth, there's been a trend to recover old musical traditions through painstaking research. The focus of attention was at first medieval and Renaissance music, which enjoyed a revival in the 1960s with pioneers like David Munrow and Noah Greenberg. Later, in the 1970s and 1980s, attention came forward in time to the Baroque and Classical eras. The process of recovery began with the text, which had to be purged of the corruptions and accretions of time. Then came the construction of the right performing tools, in terms both of technology – building old instruments – and the reconstruction of vanished performance styles with the aid of old treatises. All this allowed audiences to hear 'what the composer intended'.

As Charles Rosen tartly remarks, this method of recreating old music tends to confuse what composers wanted with what they got.[4] In the case of many composers, notably Bach, we can be pretty sure that the gulf between those two things was vast. And as Richard Taruskin has pointed out, our vision of how, say, a Baroque opera aria should sound is as much informed by modern prejudices and tastes as it is by an objective reading of what the evidence tells us. 'The whole trouble with Early Music as a movement is the way it has uncritically accepted the post-Romantic work-concept and imposed it anachronistically on pre-Romantic repertoires.'[5] This is bound to be so, as evidence always has to be interpreted. The whole idea of authenticity in early music has taken an intellectual battering in recent years. But that hasn't in any way hampered the triumphal progress of 'period performance practice', which in 30 years has moved from being a fringe movement, redolent of vegetarianism and open-toed sandals, to the dominant trend in classical music performance.

Moving on to new music, authenticity here was for decades dominated by what you could call an 'aesthetics of making'. It was the inscribing, within a text, of certain kinds of formal value. Or it was a specific sort of musical action – free improvisation, or chance procedures made in obedience to a text – where habit and convention are set aside. But, in recent decades, art music has become like other areas of music, in the sense that the criteria of authenticity have shifted to an aesthetics of reception. The focus now is on what authenticity sounds and feels like for the listener, not how it's made.

You might say: surely that must always be the case. Art music is created to be listened to, so a listener's aesthetics is what is should be judged by. But new music – of the modernist sort – has a curious way of resisting the listener's judgement. Take a piece like *Cheap Imitation* by John Cage. We hear little threadbare scraps of music, in a bleached-out idiom, poised in tone somewhere between statuesque immobility and the winsome charm of a marionette dance. It's original, to be sure. And personal too. Nobody can make pointlessness so pregnantly full as John Cage. But turn to the music as *made*, and we see at once that the material is neither personal nor original. It consists entirely of fragments of Erik Satie's *Socrate*, chopped up and rearranged.

So what we have is a divorce between making and expression. Writing a music of quirky charm was not Cage's intention in *Cheap Imitation*, any more than it was his intention to evoke the Javanese gamelan in *Sonatas and Interludes* for prepared piano. It is this severing of the expressive qualities of a piece from the composer's intention that makes discussion of modern music's expressivity so difficult. We hear the signs of certain expressive values, but something about the context, the lack of narrative 'follow-through' tells us that these signs do not make a unified subjectivity. The result is to make the charm of Cage's sonatas seem like an epiphenomenon, an accidental result of something whose real value lies elsewhere; the intellectual appeal of its mode of construction, say, or its anarchic world-view. This throws the attention of both critics and creators back, once again, to the material qualities of a piece. But that search for substance will be frustrated, because there is no real 'material', only a cheap imitation of it.

So what are we left with? Cage would say 'nothing'; but actually there is something. John Cage's music is a music of repudiation. It is a great refusal of Western art music, and the concept of goal-directedness which that music projects. In its place it puts a different vision of music, and therefore of life – a happily anarchic view, where non-intention, 'letting-go', is embraced, and art and life allowed to blend with one another.

It is the strange magic of Cage's music that it makes his great 'No' seem so eminently positive. More often in recent avant-garde music the 'No' does indeed seem negative, which is no doubt more consistent, but it turns the listeners' experience into a donning of sackcloth and ashes. In a composer like Richard Barrett, the playfulness and humour of Cage are sternly set aside. His music tries to achieve what Samuel Beckett (Barrett's intellectual mentor) achieves in literature; namely to strip away all the comforting illusions of existence, and reveal that, when thus reduced to its 'essence', the human personality is nothing more than an impotent echoing hollowness. Barrett achieves this with impressive and appalling intensity. His music fights against an inevitable downward trajectory towards extinction by vain little acts of memory and splenetic self-assertion.

There is a political dimension to Barrett's music, which seems to be as much an attack on 'bourgeois' complacency as it is a comment on a more general human condition. In this regard he is similar to the *grand maître* of the recent 'negative

turn' in modernism, Helmut Lachenmann. Lachenmann's music uses old-fashioned acoustic
media in order to deconstruct and interrogate
them. But this is not the stylistic 'deconstruction'
of a Stravinsky; it is far more thorough-going
than that, going to the roots of musical actions
and musical materials. Again, 'roots' here has
the opposite meaning to the one it has in 'roots
music', where the 'given' is celebrated as something beyond question, a source of certainty.
In Lachenmann's view music should be rooted in
uncertainty. He wants: 'a music which, in order to
be grasped, does not require a privileged intellectual training, but can rely uniquely upon its
compositional clarity and logic; a music which is
at the same time the expression and the aesthetic
form of a curiosity able to reflect everything –
including the illusion of progressiveness. Art as a
foretaste of freedom in an age of unfreedom.' And
as if that weren't forbidding enough, Lachenmann
goes on to say: 'If the act of composing is meant to
go beyond the tautological use of pre-existing
expressive forms and – as a creative act – to recall
that human potential which grants man the dignity
of a cognizant being, able to act on the basis of this
cognition, then composition is by no means a
"putting together" but rather a "taking apart",
and more: a confrontation with the interconnec-
tions and necessities of the musical substance.'[6]

You might expect the music that results to have the hard, merciless quality of the intellectual programme that impels it. But the surprising thing about Lachenmann's music is how gentle it is. When shouts or explosions do occur, they seem vain protests against a constantly encroaching silence, which seems to be the true condition of the music. The faint scratchings and rustling sounds are like the surface agitation of a silence which persists. And because everything in the music is 'taken apart' – the method of sound production as much as historical givens like melody – what one hears is often hard to place. In Lachenmann's heavily politicized setting of Hans Christian Andersen's *Little Match Seller*, one hears complexes of sounds whose origins are hard to fathom. Is that faint sound the rustling of bow-hair on a cello string, or is it electronically generated, or is it radio static?

The Utopian hopes of this aestheticized Marxism are so tremulous, so full of mute pathos, that they often seem more like hopelessness – when they don't tip over into outright nihilism, as they do in the case of Barrett, whose music seems a perfect illustration of the Psalmist's line: 'Hope long deferred maketh the heart sick.'[7] Not surprisingly, this kind of music is mainly an affair of mainland Europe. It is much rarer in Britain (indeed those composers who embrace it, like Barrett or Dillon, seem like Europeans *manqué*). And in the USA it's practically non-existent. In Anglo-Saxon countries, the attitude of repudiation is either literally anarchic (as in John Cage), or it takes the form of an exaggerated pedantry, an absurd hypertrophy of order that seems to repudiate the solemnities of the European avant-garde as much as the ghastliness of the bourgeoisie. The American composer Tom Johnson has been cheerfully sending up the pretensions of the modernists towards total order. His 'Narayana's Cows' takes the calculations of an ancient Indian mathematician of the fecundity of cows across many generations, and translates them into notes, with absurd precision. In Britain, there's an entire school of 'experimental composers' whose ranks include John White, composer of the entertaining *Drinking and Hooting Machine*, Gavin Bryars, composer of *The Squirrel and the Rickety-Rackety Bridge*, and Michael Nyman, who recomposed the catalogue aria from Mozart's *Don Giovanni* and called it *In Re Don Giovanni*. This last example shows that, in one respect at least, Nyman is more radical than the gloomy Marxists. Lachenmann, with few exceptions, insists on generating his own material, as a first step towards authenticity. From the experimentalists' point of view, that makes the result too entangled with the creator's personality. Distance is what's needed.

What both of these approaches – the modernist/ nihilist and the joyously experimental – have in common is a determination to avoid anything like expressivity. But as we've seen in the example of Cage's *Cheap Imitation*, that very avoidance itself has expressive consequences. This is the ironic fate that lies in wait for a musical practice where the aesthetics of 'making' and the aesthetics of 'receiving' are so completely divorced from one another.

The very same ironic fate has visited the other great modernist tradition, the tradition of Schoenberg, Boulez, Xenakis, Carter. The attitude of this tradition toward expressivity could be summed up by the remark of the painter Georges Seurat: 'Some people have done me the honour of finding beauty in what I do, but I paint by my method with no other thought in mind.' Likewise, these composers compose by their method with no other thought in mind. But nevertheless the music takes on expressive qualities, qualities which the audience cannot help but read as meant by the composer. Just as Lachenmann's repudiation yields a fragile beauty, so Elliott Carter's ingenious play with notes yields a tense exuberance.

In one sense Elliott Carter (aged 95 and still composing at the time of writing) is just as 'anti' as Cage or Lachenmann, in the sense that his music refuses any easy identification between sounds and expression. But Carter has none of

Lachenmann's gloom or suspicion of music's material. Carter takes the straightforward view that notes – not wispy sounds and scratchings – can bear the most complicated thoughts and ideas. His sketches – thousands of pages for big pieces like the Symphony of Three Orchestras – swarm with all the possible permutations of a few germinating intervals and chords. You won't find sadness expressed by minor chords, or joy expressed by major ones and rip-roaring climaxes. Nonetheless, one can hear and feel those emotions in the music, expressed in a way that often communicates at an instinctive level. Even Roger Scruton, that fierce critic of modernism in music, has to concede that Carter's Concert for Orchestra (1969) 'succeeds in turning an uncompromising modernism to the service of joy'.[8]

Joy is Carter's dominant mood, but it's not so much a feeling as a state of mental exuberance. The melodies and harmonies barely register in themselves – here and there you might catch a chord with a particular pungent sonority, but you won't have more than a millisecond to enjoy it. What really counts is the agreeably fizzing sensation of a myriad connections being made. The music moves at the speed of thought itself, and as long as it lasts, it gives the listener the pleasing sense of being as clever as the composer. At the opposite extreme are pieces like the 'Adagio Tenebroso' from the recent *Symphonia* where, at length, a kind of melancholy distils itself from a procession of vast towering sonorities moving with giant slowness. I say 'a kind of melancholy' because the music's expressiveness is more to do with types of being, and types of change, than they are with more codifiable emotions. The melancholy is a second-order expressiveness, which supervenes on more immediately audible things like slowness and vastness.

You hear a similar kind of 'formalized' expressivity in all those younger composers who acknowledge Carter as a mentor. Oliver Knussen's *Coursing* may be inspired by Niagara Falls, but there are none of the clichés of 'wateriness' in music, no rippling added sixth chords and sevenths *à la* Ravel. What Knussen's music does is to metaphorize the physical reality of a waterfall, the transformation from surging and falling foam to broad, peaceful movement. On the face of it, it seems a curious idea to represent the physical reality of water in music, rather than its poetic meaning for us as humans. But for these composers, true expression means escaping from convention, and the best of way to achieve that is to change the focus of the expressive project, from subject to object. And even when the subject is the focus, 'feeling' is treated in a way more akin to perception. Carter himself makes this clear when he compares the sound of his music to watching a landscape from above during flight.

The notion that in our time subjectivity dissolves into bundles of sensations, and that these fleeting patches of experience should be the proper focus of music, is a leitmotif in this brand of new music. Here, authenticity means being true to our experience, and not taking refuge in reach-me-down gestures of feeling, what Lachenmann calls 'the tautological use of pre-existing forms'. You find the same fierce, almost moral urge to drive to the root of things in the so-called 'spectral' music of French composers like Gérard Grisey. His *Partiels* begins with a ferociously loud and gritty bass E, whose 'dirty' tone-colour is then analysed into its constituent parts by the treble instruments. The expressive effect is one of mysterious enlightenment, as if the hidden reality of sounds is being revealed to us (the title actually refers to the physical reality of instrumental timbres, which consist of a fundamental tone, the one which gives the note its pitch, and a host of higher 'partials' which register subliminally as colour). That process of revelation eventually generates a kind of musical logic and continuity, as the coruscating murmur of 'partials' spin themselves out into a new pattern. This new pattern implies a new 'fundamental', which in turn generates new 'partials', and so on.

This 'spinning out' of course owes nothing to acoustics; it is generated by the composer's intention, though Grisey spins the music with such subtlety that it really does seem as if the piece is creating itself out of its own substance. But to praise the music in those terms immediately suggests a connection with older and more familiar forms of music. When we want to praise a Mozart or Brahms symphony do we not often say that the piece sounds inevitable, as if it *had* to unfold in precisely this way? The success of Grisey's piece is eloquent proof that it transcends its own programme. This is no mere transcription of a physical process; it is a musical *metaphor* for that process, and therefore crosses the magic line between transcription and expression.

Expression, though, can only exist where there is some connection with music's past. It is this fraught relationship with the past, denied at the level of overt intention, but subtly reinstated by the music itself, that makes modernist music so interesting. Knussen's *Coursing* may not use the clichés of musical 'wateriness' but it certainly refers obliquely to them. Somewhere in the incandescent sonorities of that piece, the memory of Ravel's *Jeux d'eaux* can be felt and heard. The watchword, always, is obliquity. When a reference to older music does become audible in the music – for example, when the solo horns in Julian Anderson's *Imagin'd Corners* suggest the world of German Romanticism – it has to be oblique and fleeting, the reference vanishing as soon as its made.

At its best, this glittering, restless, fleet form of music can excite the heart and mind like no other. But in a composer working at less than full stretch, its dangers become apparent. Obliquity can turn into a kind of preciousness. The refusal of the music ever to assert strong beats, the extreme elaboration of texture and dynamics, generates a kind of 'aesthetics of avoidance' which can be debilitating. The danger has always been there in modernist music. Schoenberg, when he elaborated his 'twelve-note' method of composing, declared that its aim was to establish a total democracy among the notes, and banish any idea of tonal centre. But when it came to actual composing, he couldn't resist fashioning twelve-note rows which were full of tonal references – references which the music had to both embrace (otherwise why would they be there?) and deny (because this was, after all, a twelve-note piece). 70 years on, one finds the same tension in Oliver Knussen's Whitman settings, whose entire material is derived from a five-note figure which has clear tonal implications. The music itself can't decide whether to embrace or deny those implications. But rather than a fruitful ambiguity, the technical contortions Knussen indulges in to avoid the implications of his own material create a sense of agonized carefulness, like a man trying not to step on his own shadow.

By now a pattern has revealed itself in these various authenticities. World music is the odd one out, in that authenticity there is bound up with the expression of a culture from within. A Malian *griot* is a true 'voice of the people' in a way that Western musicians can only dream of. In the West authenticity tends to mean quite the opposite; it means being *against* the taste of the majority, that taste being something that has become some-how corrupt. In so-called 'early music' what was corrupt was the performing tradition, which had to be restored to its roots. The idea that authen-ticity is to do with going back to some primal state of purity is also found in jazz, though it has its opponents too.

In modern music authenticity could be restora-tive (as in Schoenberg) or revolutionary (as in Boulez or Cage). Either way, it was bound up with a positive vision of musical material, imbued with formally created meanings. 'The notes them-selves' were what mattered. But in recent decades that formal criterion has faded, and what has moved gradually to the fore is a stance of being 'anti'. What much new music is 'against' is being consumable: it abhors the 'tautological use of pre-existing expressive forms'. If that abhorrence is shown by the Lachenmann method of the 'taking apart and putting together' of material then we're still in the sphere of art music. But if it's manifested by an expressive path – a 'going to extremes' in terms of gesture, noise, violence – then there's nothing about the music that results which ties it necessarily to the art sphere. That kind of 'anti' stance can be found in many areas, from punk to John Zorn. So the question we posed earlier in the chapter has to be answered 'yes and no'. In some areas of art music, 'authenticity' is still bound up with a conception of musical material, a musical realm, just as it was in the nineteenth century (the fact that, in Barrett's or Lachenmann's case, this material is really the musical equivalent of anti-matter doesn't alter that). But in other areas, the 'anti' stance is rooted in expressive gestures of repudiation and anger.

The expressive route to authenticity has certain advantages. If old forms are invoked and then 'pushed to extremes' then the audience's musical expectations and knowledge will be called upon, and challenged, rather than simply denied. But this is a tricky path to take – because once you embrace tonal forms of expression, you may find your music doesn't sound so very different to those composers who don't share your 'anti' stance, and who just want to write the kind of music that people enjoy. The question whether it's possible to preserve authenticity while embracing all the things authenticity in new music wants to reject – tradition, memory, tonality – is the subject we must now turn to.

NOTES

1. *Village Voice*, July 2000.
2. Songlines presents World Music Manteca CD 202.
3. Cook, R. (2001). *Blue Note Records: The Biography*. London, Secker & Warburg, p. 12.
4. Rosen, C. (2000). 'The Benefits of Authenticity' in *Critical Entertainments*. Cambridge, MA, Harvard University Press, p. 202.
5. Taruskin, R. (1995). *Text and Act*. Oxford, Oxford University Press, p. 13.
6. Hausler, J. (ed) (1996). *Helmut Lachenmann – Musik als existentielle Erfahrung: Schriften 1966–1995*. Trans Roger Clément (see http://www.brietkopf.com/komponisten_essay).
7. The Italian composer Luigi Nono best captures this quality. The title of one of his later pieces sets the tone: 'La lontananza nostalgica utopica futura', 'The Nostalgic Distance of a Utopian Future'.
8. Scruton, R. (1997). *The Aesthetics of Music*. Oxford, Clarendon Press, p. 494.

7

❧

Expression Makes
a Comeback

According to one view of the history of modern music, it's an easy question to answer. Memory, tradition, and tonality aren't just compatible with authenticity – they are its *sine qua non*, the very things that give authenticity substance and lift it beyond empty gestures of repudiation and anger. They are the only things which can ensure that music is indeed *music*, and not merely an array of sounds, meaningful only to its creator.

This conservative view of modern music certainly has public opinion on it's side. Ask concert-goers or CD buyers what classical music they enjoy from the last half-century, and the chances are they'll name Britten and Shostakovich rather than Boulez. Ask them what art music of the present day they listen to, and they're much more likely to name John Tavener, or John Corigliano, or John Adams, or James Macmillan, than they are Richard Barrett or Birtwistle or Elliott Carter. This proves, according to the conservatives, that the true history of modern music is the one re-pressed by the textbooks, and by the musical and academic establishment.

The same accusation of censorship could be levelled at this book. Why, thus far, has so much space been devoted here to Boulez and Birtwistle, and none to Britten or Shostakovich? A short answer is that the music of Britten and Shostako-vich doesn't stand in need of explication. At a certain level of understanding, their music is obvious; it uses a musical vocabulary which will not puzzle anyone who's followed music as far as the early twentieth century. Whereas modernist music presents a baffling face, which only becomes readable when approached with a certain imagi-native sympathy.

It might seem, though, that in bestowing such an effort of sympathy on modernist music, I'm also withholding it from the other sorts of music that don't follow the modernist path. By setting up the modernist ethos as the touchstone of integrity in music, I seem to be relegating all those tonal composers that people actually enjoy to the status of also-rans, the ones who flunked the modernist challenge. This is certainly not my intention. But I do feel that the evolution of art music has a certain logic which is most starkly revealed when dealing with modernist composers. And if there is a logic in modern music's unfolding, born out of its historical situation and certain aspects of its 'stuff' (these two working in mysterious collusion) then it must follow that this logic will reveal itself across the entire art music realm. It follows because the composers working within it all started from the same global situation. They all faced music's new, disquieting 'multiplicity', they could all hear, and feel, the resultant strain in the language they'd inherited. So it must be the case that the same fault-lines, the same tensions, must be as evident in contemporary tonal music, as in contemporary modernist music. If they're not discernible there, then the anti-modernists will be proved right; the obsessive desire of people like Boulez to remake music from scratch would turn out to be the private obsessions of a cultish group of people, with no more general cultural import than the obsessions of any other sort of cult.

That is precisely the view of cultural conservatives, who see no such tensions or difficulties in the conservative, tonal music of the twentieth and early twenty-first century. How could there be, when – according to them – the language on which this music is based arises out of Nature itself? That language is the tonal system, which appears to be 'natural' in two senses. On the one hand, you have the physics of resonating bodies, which yields a purely rational basis for our perception of intervals which sound consonant and relaxed, and intervals which seem harsh and tense. And on the other, you have the seeming ubiquity of those intervals as basic building blocks in every musical tradition there's ever been. In every culture, you find the octave, the fifth, the third as the basic intervals. Likewise, you find the same basic rhythmic patterns, rooted in certain very basic somatic and motor factors of the human being – above all the division of time into 'upbeats' and 'downbeats', following the in-out rhythm of human breath, and the left-right alternation of walking and running.

When body, mind, and number ratios all seem to point towards the adoption of certain primitive units of music, it's tempting to see the tonal language of the 'common practice' as nothing more than the gradual revelation, through time, of an unchanging, objective reality. This is not the place to delve into the deep question of whether tonality is a historical construct or a given. Suffice it to say that the evidence is at best ambiguous. If the dynamic system of Western tonality were an inevitable outgrowth of the physics of intervals, and their perceptual correlatives in terms of 'euphonious' and 'cacophonous', you'd expect every musical culture to have discovered it. Whereas tonality in the strict sense is a very limited phenomenon, being found only in the West from about 1600 onwards. The fact that almost every other culture has now eagerly adopted the Western system isn't proof that, after all, tonality really is rooted in nature. What it proves is that those cultures have now thrown in their lot with modernity. The common ground is a historical dynamic, not some unchanging law of nature.

That dynamic at the beginning of the modern era was, as we've seen, one of dissolution from within, and invasion (or, if you prefer, friendly cross-fertilization) from without. The resulting convulsion in music's 'realm' could not leave anyone or anything within it untouched. This does not mean that tonality became obsolete; but it did mean that its rules, its grammar could no longer be treated as laws of nature. Suddenly the truth about them, which is that they were in large part conventional, was starkly revealed. And when a convention becomes revealed *as* conventional, it acquires a nimbus of 'pastness', it becomes something a composer uses for its associations and its expressive value. And when that happens, the musical fabric no longer presents itself as an unbroken whole, made out of the same stuff. It becomes discontinuous, a patchwork, which in some parts appears to be a genuine discourse – i.e. made up of things related to each other through a genuine syntax – and in other parts, made up of objects which stand out from the discourse, radiating their own peculiar expressive energy. These are disruptive, which is why, to a composer of a modernist cast who wants music to be genuinely unified, so much neo-tonal music is reprehensible. Take the famous moment in Berg's Violin Concerto when a chorale by Bach floats magically to the surface of the music. Berg exerts all his skill to make this expressive object seem like part of a genuine discourse, to the extent of having the last three notes of his Schoenbergian 'note-row' map exactly onto the first three notes of Bach's melody. But Boulez isn't persuaded. He describes the incursion as 'a dramatic gesture ... I do not think it a very profound gesture – indeed I find rather that it expresses anxiety'.[1]

Displaying the signs of neurosis isn't necessarily disabling to an artwork (Boulez clearly doesn't think so, otherwise he wouldn't conduct Berg's concerto quite as often as he does). Nor does the alienation from tonal gestures and forms that modernism produces necessarily carry a charge of regret and nostalgia. In Stravinsky that distance is a cause for joy, something he takes good care to preserve. He skews and distorts the old syntax just enough to make conventional turns of phrase and the simple building blocks of tonality seem richly strange. The distorting is carried across the whole texture, so that in the end it becomes a new norm. Nothing stands out from the discourse like a quotation (not even the real quotations from Rossini in *Jeux de Cartes*, which are witty but entirely without that 'pathos of distance' we find in Berg).

One reason Stravinsky's achievement is so miraculous, and so joyous, is that it gives us such a convincing simulacrum of the old unified musical realm. But, in the end, it is only a simulacrum. A distortion of an old rule doesn't constitute a genuinely new rule, which is why Stravinsky's music hasn't yielded a genuine new 'common practice', only a 'manner' (which is why Schoenberg loathed it, and why Boulez loathes it today). So it's only to be expected that the numerous Stravinsky-imitators sound mannered (as the composer put it, 'what they imitate is not my music but my *person* in my music'). In different ways, all the tonal music written in the first two-thirds of the twentieth century shows this gradual usurping of 'grammar' by 'manner', meaning a personal set of gestures and mannerisms which evoke the expressive power of tonal vocabulary, without obeying the grammar that used to bind that vocabulary together. The result, in Britten and Shostakovich no less than in Berg, is that tonality starts to become privatized, its means linked to certain emotional states of particular importance to that composer. For example in Britten, major chords when arranged in particular conjunctions, and associated with particular tone-colours (harps, boys' voices), mean unspoilt innocence. In Shostakovich a certain kind of strident dissonance against a strutting tonic-dominant vamp refers to the brutalization that totalitarianism produces. Tonal music turns out to be no less 'multiple' than modernist music; which is another way of saying that it, too, is modern music, underneath the appearance of familiarity.

If that is true of the first generation of 'modern tonal' composers, how much more true it is of tonal composers now living. Here the lived connection with the 'common practice' of c.1600–1900 has vanished, and what we have is a conscious revivalism, with all the distortion of distance and uncertainty of tone that implies. In some cases the adoption of tonal means following a kind of conversion experience, in which a composer 'sees the light' after spending years writing modernist music. This rhythm, whereby a style adopted with fervent conviction is then repudiated and replaced by a new one (the process perhaps repeated more than once) is itself quintessentially modern, and another sign that 'new tonality' and modernism are really brothers under the skin.

There are many ways tonality can be reinvented, all of which involve a difficult marriage of 'going back' to some particular, style-laden example of tonality with some formal reinvention of tonality's rules. The results may be impressive, but there's bound to be a sense of strain. Going back to a tradition, recovering a language, can never yield the easy sense of belonging and mastery possessed by those born into it. This sense of rupture is hardly recent. Even for Brahms, that sense of easy possession was under threat, and had to be bolstered by research, antiquarianism, the cultivation of obsolete techniques; none of which were needed by Mozart.

But the sense of rupture for someone like John Adams is much more profound. And he, like John Tavener, like Arvo Pärt, like Alfred Schnittke, like Rochberg, like Robin Holloway, had to find his way back to traditional means after much soul-searching. What that means in each of those composers is, though, vastly different. The way back may lead to a total repudiation of modernism. Or it may lead to a curious marriage of modernism and traditional forms, or even a see-sawing back and forth between them. The change can be sudden, or it can be gradual, as it was in the case of John Adams. His is a fascinating case, because his music seems not so much a reaction to modernism, as a transforming of it from within. He uses the devices of modernism to subvert it.

That sounds like an impossibility, if the model of modernism you're using is Boulez or Elliott Carter. There's no way that their musical idioms could be married with tonal ways of thinking. The two sorts of discourses are utterly incompatible. Unlike, say, the serial music of Schoenberg, which is thoroughly imbued with memories of nineteenth century Austro-German music; which was evidence, for Boulez, that Schoenberg bottled out of his own musical revolution. (One of the ways

Boulez likes to mock Schoenberg is to play the first few bars of his Violin Concerto, with the solo part harmonized *à la* Brahms. The fact that he can do it so easily shows just how far Schoenberg's 'music of the future' is compromised by the past. You couldn't do the same party trick with any piece by Boulez.)

There is, though, a kind of modernism which has proved to be all too amenable to being captured by expressivity. It's called minimalism. This is surprising, because on first hearing, the early works of Steve Reich and Philip Glass and Terry Riley are anything but expressive. Take Reich's *Piano Phase* of 1968. We hear a little phrase in even semiquavers obsessively pattered out on a piano, which after a while seems to be afflicted with a stutter. Only after a few more bars does it become clear what's happening. The phrase is actually being played by two pianos, one of which has speeded ahead very slowly, creating a momentary rhythmic chaos. After a few more seconds order is restored, as the pianos move back into phase. But melodically they're out of synch, as one piano is now exactly one step ahead of the first.

The fact that this process is repeated over and over, with not the faintest hint of development or change, marks it out as belonging to a certain kind of modernism. What counts is the purity of the musical process, which must be worked out with iron consistency. The music never seems to become aware of itself; it never develops a memory of its own past, and so is never moved to alter its trajectory. And we, the listeners, are left out of the count; our contribution is the minimal one of spotting the process. Minimalism is unnerving in the way it reduces us to a bare perceptual apparatus; memory, judgement, sensibility, imagination, are all superfluous to requirements. There's the same remorseless working out of a preordained scheme in Philip Glass's *Music in Twelve Parts*, where an ensemble of voices, electric organs and saxophones presents repeating patterns in an unvarying flat dynamic and tempo.

It might be wondered why anyone should enjoy a music which sets out to cancel subjectivity so effectively. In fact that cancelling is precisely the attraction. It's pleasant to be given a holiday from oneself, to feel the normal darting activity of one's mental and emotional life soothed by the minimalist tick and euphonious chords. Thus soothed, we enjoy the changing process without looking for anything more. What minimal music (of the hard-line, late 1960s sort) bestows is a marvellous 'lightness of being'.

This seems an unlikely soil to nurture expressivity of any kind. But actually the passage from the wide-eyed, day-glo blankness of Glass to the heartfelt expressivity of Adams' *El Dorado* is not as vast as it appears. The raw material of early minimalism outlines a type of cool, laid-back harmony – lots of flattened sevenths and added sixths – which has a considerable overlap with the popular realm. The jazz-rock of Weather Report, rock bands like Steely Dan and a piece like Steve Reich's *Music for Eighteen* all belong recognizably to the same culture. So although, at the time, early minimalism seemed as pure as a piece of Boulezian 'total serialism', in retrospect it's clear that it had many ties to a wider musical realm. It was open to history, which is why the subsequent histories of these two modernisms have been so different. The Boulezian variety is still locked up in its bunker (although there are signs, in younger French composers like Marc-André Dalbavie, that it's finally going the American way).

That connection with familiar harmonic idioms allowed a feature of minimalism to emerge which might have forever remained hidden. This is its tendency to sentimentality. This might sound an odd thing to say of an idiom so apparently chilly. But the link (apart from chilliness itself – the warmth of sentimentality is only an illusion) is obsessiveness. As Germaine Greer keeps reminding us, obsessiveness is a peculiarly male trait, and the fact that all the minimalist composers are male does seem to bear out her theory. Obsessiveness is an inability, or perhaps a refusal, to see things in the round, and that imperviousness to the world also marks out sentimentality. In musical terms, obsessiveness means the thorough-going mechanization of music (and note the contrast with the Boulez form of modern music, whose doubts, hesitations, and endless elaborations and revisings are anything but mechanical). Sentimentality means the pursuit of an emotional trajectory outlined at the beginning, without hesitation or deviation, where the pleasurable experience of emotion – the 'feeling of feeling' – becomes its own justification. What prevented the formal monomania of minimalism from tipping over into sentimentality was the narrowness of the harmonic language, which couldn't venture much beyond a kind of louche spaciousness, redolent of speed and wide-open spaces (Reich's *Music for Eighteen* is, in addition to being a masterpiece, the perfect road-movie sound-track).

Then came John Adams, the composer who would lead minimalism out of its self-made wilderness. He was, and is, a composer of enormous gifts, with a harmonic palette that embraces Brahms, Schoenberg, jazz, Broadway. But the core of that palette is still that road-movie tonality, at once rich (the chords are full of piled up added-notes – sixths, sevenths, elevenths, thirteenths) and loose (there are no 'leading notes', so that sense of tight, ineluctable logic you get in tonal harmony is missing).

The 'logic' of tonality, though, is exactly what gives it its quality of being 'musical material', i.e. something that is to a degree autonomous, free to follow its own laws. Get rid of that, and tonality loses its freedom. It becomes entirely the creature of the composer, obliged to follow his or her expressive purposes. This is exactly what we find in the second movement of Adams' *El Dorado*. We hear the exact working out, again without hesitation or deviation, of a programme outlined in the composer's liner notes; the emergence, from the primordial miasma, of living nature, which burgeons into glorious, teeming variety. The piece is one of Adams' most successful precisely because it never has to deal with ambiguity; the trajectory is an unbroken straight line. What makes that trajectory even more irresistible is that there is, lurking behind the swelling emotive harmonies, the almost-hidden hand of minimalism. Ticking away in the background is that relentless rhythm, just as it ticks away in Reich's *Four Organs*. It is characteristic of minimalism that its rhythmic life can never be implied, never be generated from within the music's discourse, because implication implies the collaboration of a thinking, feeling subject – the very thing that minimalism works so hard to deny. It has to be insistently overt, 'extrinsic', plastered on to the music from the outside.

I don't mean to imply that anyone who works in this emotive, post-minimal language is a cynical manipulator. On the contrary, what marks out Adams is his overwhelming sincerity, which leads him to embrace risky causes. But his music reminds one of Stravinsky's wise saying that 'sincerity is the *sine qua non* which at the same time guarantees nothing'. The critical problem with Adams is a problem in the language itself, which confuses sincerity of purpose with the abolition of anything like an objectifying distance from the material (and which thereby abolishes 'material' itself). Because it works on its listeners at two levels – the bodily level, coerced by the ticking rhythm, and the mental, coerced by the swellingly emotive vocabulary – it doesn't require their collaboration. One has two choices, to surrender or resist. I suspect Adams is aware of this problem. Each new piece tries to increase the distance between himself and his minimalist heritage, but even in the Violin Concerto, one of his most subtle scores, its deadening hand can be felt. The problem is that in a piece where he does forswear that heritage entirely, like the *Wound Dresser*, one is left with a reach-me-down 1940s expressivity which sounds like Samuel Barber without the tunes.

The problem of how to find a truly contemporary voice in the realm of art music is one that troubles American music now – leaving aside Elliott Carter who is still serenely convinced by the modernist view of the world that gripped him in the 1940s. But the fact that Carter has practically no audience or followers in America – he is to all intents and purposes a European composer – shows how irrelevant his music is to the temper of his own country. David Lang is much more symptomatic of that temper, and like many younger American composers, such as Michael Dougherty, he tries to co-opt the idioms of popular music directly, without passing through the constructivist filter of minimalism. The result in a way is more refreshing, but the same problem, of a lurking tendency to sentimentality, still lies in wait. However it takes a rather different form. In post-minimal music it's to do with the obsessiveness of the material, combined with an overt intention to 'express'. With David Lang, it's more to do with the dangers attending a certain kind of 'tough' stance. Toughness can be as sentimental as any other expressive quality, if it's unmodulated by a discourse which modulates it, questions it. Without that, it's all too liable to flip into its opposite, just as it does with 'tough guys' in real life. Lang's piece *Under Orpheus* shows that he is indeed the James Cagney of new music; tough on the outside, marshmallow on the inside.

'Toughness' takes on a different meaning in someone like the Russian (or rather Soviet) composer Alfred Schnittke. Here it's the listener who has to be tough, to stay the course. The composer is anything but tough; on the contrary, he seems in his music like a person with no protection, naked before the blows meted out by the world.

These were legion; Schnittke was a composer of German-Jewish extraction, with an urgent need to write a new, experimental form of music that broke the official socialist-realist mould. All those things ensured that his musical career in the Soviet Union would be obstructed at every point. Being a kind of exile in his own country exacerbated Schnittke's natural tendency to view the composer's role as that of mourner for a past when musical language, the subjective needs of the composer, and society's expectations all seemed made for each other. Schnittke was aware of the difficulty of creating a unified artwork in the modern, deracinated world, but he cannot regard this with the easy-going irony of a Western composer. For him this is an agonizing situation, which his music attempts to overcome – though from the beginning we hear a kind of despairing foreknowledge of the failure of that attempt.

Schnittke has his own way of 'going to extremes'. In Lachenmann, it's to do with interrogating the inherited characteristics of 'material'; in Glass, it's a hypertrophy of system; in Schnittke, it's an extreme of expressivity, where conventional signs of expressivity are pushed to the point where they sound unhinged. In the Viola Concerto, there's a point where the soloist launches a phrase that, 150 ago, was conventionally expressive of yearning. With its Italianate melodic turn leading to a sighing dissonance, it sounds like something from an early Wagner opera. It's repeated up a step, which is also a conventional move. But the move happens again, and again, and again, the dynamic and expressive intensity increasing all the while. Well before the viola reaches a screaming pitch of altitude and intensity, we've come to realize that what was conventional has become pathological. Another disturbing tendency in Schnittke is the sudden irruption, into a modernist texture full of turbid dissonance, of something sweetly innocent, as if a passage from an unknown work by Mozart had simply parachuted into the piece from above. Or you might find a series of hammer-blow common chords, like a Baroque concerto grosso, gradually poisoned by dissonance (as happens in the Concerto Grosso no.1).

The pathological aspect of Schnittke's music, its refusal to ameliorate its shocking contrasts, makes it one of the few kinds of contemporary music which really deserves that over-used epithet, 'challenging'. By the end of a Schnittke piece, one feels as if one's nerves have been rubbed raw. There are many other composers who make a similar bid to reach the 'naked flesh of emotion' as Debussy described it (though his means were utterly different, to do with hints and subtle shades). In James Macmillan there's a similar violent juxtaposition of utterly dissimilar musics. But you only have to hear a few bars of a piece like *The Confessions of*

Isobel Goudie to realize that his intentions are really very different. Towards the end of that piece we hear a keening sound in the strings, representing the final moments of Goudie before her execution for witchcraft. Eventually the axe falls, in a series of orchestral hammer-blows, while the keening continues unperturbed by all this violence. This example is a *locus classicus* of the way, in recent years, modernist discoveries have been co-opted to anti-modern purposes. The idea that music need not be a unity, that it could be made of parts that proceed in ignorance of each other, was one of the great discoveries of the postwar modernists. It was anti-subjective, anti-expressive in its intention. But in Macmillan's piece the effect is full of pathos; the injustice of the verdict on Goudie, and her piteous death, are simply 'expressed' in a new way. The means may be different, but the relation between idea and musical material is basically a nineteenth-century one.

This seizing of modernist devices like clusters, discontinuity, dissonance for romantically expressive purposes is becoming a widespread, if not dominant, trend in new music. You hear it in a piece like Corigliano's First Symphony, whose first movement commemorates a pianist friend who died of AIDS. At several points we hear an off-stage piano playing Albéniz's famous tango, a piece of which this friend was especially fond. For me the expressive intentions of this moment, and of the hammer-blows in Macmillan's piece, are too nakedly revealed. The whole being of these moments is absorbed in the intention to wring our hearts; there's no real 'substance' underneath which subsists apart from the feeling which is conveyed. This is the essential difference with, say, the terrifying whirlwind which begins the last movement of Beethoven's Ninth Symphony. Take away the expressive aspect of that music, and you have plenty of substance left; a particular kind of severe dissonance, a set of rhythms, a trumpet figure of a distinct martial cast, and, over-all, a harmonic movement from tonic to dominant. You have, in short, a discourse. And it is the presence of that objective substratum which makes the music genuinely *musical*. The Macmillan and the Corigliano have no discourse; they are both pure gesture.

But why should this matter? And isn't this putting the cart before the horse; why not allow the effectiveness of the music as expression to determine whether or not it is musical? The danger with that approach is that once you identify music with expressivity you open the door to sentimentality. Sentimentality in music, as in everything, is the severing of emotion from true perception – two things which have to be in constant touch to prevent one or the other from falling into pathology. Feeling tells us what is worth attending to in the world. But the act of attending then modulates, or even reverses, the feeling. It is by watching and listening closely, and thinking and feeling about what is in front of us – rather than about some agreeable fantasy – that separates true from false feeling. Reality both encourages our feelings and reins them in.

In music, the thing that does duty for 'reality' is indeed *music*; the stuff of melodies, harmonies, rhythms – and perhaps also densities and complexes – on which I keep insisting. To banish musical substance, as traditionally defined, to search for a new sort of substance, or a new sort of musical action which displaces substance from its dominant position, may be an enterprise fraught with difficulty (indeed you could say it is formally self-contradictory). But at least these attempts preserve the integrity of the musical enterprise. Whereas to pillage the modernist 'canon' for usefully expressive sounds and gestures seems disreputable. That of course is not how Macmillan sees it; he thinks he's doing modern music a favour, by pulling it out of its new music ghetto. His relation to modernism is an odd mixture of embarrassment and desire. He's embarrassed by the ideological and intellectual convictions of modernist music, but he wants the expressive *frisson* of its gestures – things like sudden violent cluster chords, *glissandi*, a 'denatured' orchestral sound where the cultural origins of instruments are lost. Macmillan stands to Boulez rather as

Tony Blair stands to an 'old Labour' ideologue like Tony Benn; it's a case of legitimation by association, rather than a real sharing of belief.

Viewed from one angle, Schnittke and Macmillan are poles apart. One pushes normal expressive gestures to a pathological degree of intensity, the other embeds modernist gestures in an ameliorating context, which neuters their dangerous disruptive power (they meekly accept the expressive label the composer pins on them: a collage of short downward *glissandi means* 'Celtic keening', dissonant crashes in a quiet context *mean* the individual crushed by arbitrary authority, and so on). But they have one important thing in common. The gestures are made to appear the natural bearers of their meanings, as if convention had been banished.

Once those gestures become repeated, though, they very quickly become conventional themselves. The role of convention in new music is hard to assess, because it's one of those terms, like 'dramatic' or 'symphonic', which have been more-or-less evacuated of meaning. In that vacant space you now find a neat conflation of catch-all description and summary judgement. So – as mentioned above – 'symphonic' now refers, not to a specific musical form, but to anything played by an orchestra. 'Dramatic' no longer means a theatrical action obeying certain rules, but anything on stage that freezes the blood and melts the heart, or preferably both. Plus a vague sense of approval; to describe a new piece of music as 'dramatic' is one way of saying it's good. Likewise the word 'conventional' is now merely a short-hand way of saying that something lacks originality, and is therefore bad.

This is very curious, because not so long ago to describe a work of music (whether art or 'folk') as 'conventional' was to say no more than that it really was a piece of music, or song, and not a cack-handed approximation to one. Conventionality was simply a condition of intelligibility. To see that you only have to think of the conventional cadence that ends a Mozart symphony or a Cole Porter song. That harmonic movement doesn't express the sense of an ending, it enacts it, just as the word 'hello' enacts a greeting.

But as music became progressively loosened from social function, its ability to 'enact' things in an uncomplicated, implicit way became eroded. It was a process aided and abetted by the Romantics, for whom convention was the enemy. Charles Rosen has shown how, behind the strange new colours, the surprising forms, and the wayward chromatic harmony of Romantic music, lay a dream: the dream of a music totally without convention, that would communicate in a direct 'unmediated' way.[2] The dream was finally realized in the twentieth century, firstly by the Dadaists and Surrealists, later by all those composers who embraced the aesthetic of the Happening and the chance event.

Because the traditional relationship between composer, player and society has proved so hard to subvert, the battle to be original, to escape convention, has had to be fought entirely in the domain of 'the purely musical'. This is why in a modernist piece there can be no reliance on routine, no use of pre-set forms like sonata form, no use of 'pre-fab' material of the sort that makes up a good 80 per cent of a Mozart sonata. Everything must be new. But what modernist music shows is that when convention is pushed out of the front door it comes right in again at the back. Contemporary music – of the modernist kind, at least – is full of things that appear, at first sight, to be something like conventions. Here are some of them:

1. a rhythmic style that studiously avoids the beat, resulting in a texture that – to an ear unused to the idiom – is worryingly fluid, the rhythmic equivalent of a Dalí watch. Good example – the beginning of the Chamber Concerto by the Hungarian composer György Ligeti.
2. the 'fade-in' and 'fade-out' ending. At one time this was almost as ubiquitous as the

'fanfare' style opening was in the Italian Baroque concerto. The music creeps in out of nothing, and returns to it (though more often, one finds these used separately). You find it firstly in the great early modernist works like Debussy's *Jeux*, or Berg's First Orchestral Piece of 1910. A good later example would be Elliott Carter's Double Concerto. The fade-out is something classical music shares with pop music, and it shows that, vastly different though they are in almost every way, the 'grammar' of pop and new classical have one thing in common: a difficulty in bringing things to an emphatic closure. (Though seen from another angle they're very different. The pop music fade-out is found only on disc, never in live performance, and its role is partly to make the listener hang in there for the next track.)

3. the 'sneeze'. A gesture embodied by giving a longish note a big crescendo, ending in a sudden cut-off climax. Often an array of sneezes might be arranged in layers, each climaxing at different points. Example: Harrison Birtwistle's *Verses for Ensembles*. This gesture, apparently so trivial, is important because it's a synecdoche of the body language of modernist music: athletic, weightless, 'spiritualized' ('pneuma' taken in and expelled), living on its nerve-ends.

4. an absence of movements – pieces happen in a single unbroken span, usually of around 15–20 minutes.
6. lots of percussion.

Between *c*.1955 and 1985 literally hundreds of pieces were written which showed at least some of these features. They were all a way of annulling the conventions of earlier classical music, but by the 1980s they had themselves become conventional, something to be rebelled against. Late 1960s minimalism was the first sign of that rebellion (though, as we've seen, it was deeply modernist in its method). In younger, post-minimalist composers, the iron-clad method of early minimalism has gone, but the polemical thrust remains. A piece like Steve Martland's *Horses of Instruction* with its lack of expression marks, its constant loud tempo, its bright, primary colours and emphatic beat, is anti-modernist through and through.

However, the fact that modernism hardened into an orthodoxy obscures the fact that its conventions – its turns of phrase, its gestures, including those listed above – are profoundly different to those in Mozart or Haydn. They are engendered by the very struggle to escape convention, and that paradoxical state of being reveals itself in the air of perpetual strenuousness which pervades modernist music.

This fact reveals a larger truth about new music, which is the difficulty it has in finding a healthy, sane relationship to the past. A convention, in the old sense, was a perfect example of sanity and health. It was the release, into the present moment, of the stored-up potential of a phrase elaborated by age-old practice, in an action at once conscious and instinctive, chosen and 'inevitable'. It is that mysterious dual aspect which allows Mozart's banal material to sound richly meaningful. Deprived of that dual aspect, modern composers (or rather those modern composers with a conscience) have to fight the natural tendency of musical substance to fall into mere gesture. Thus the tendency to choose those varieties of gesture – notably the fade-out ending – which can be given a fantastically elaborate formal dress. The elaboration comes from the tendency noted above, to collapse expressivity into the mimicking of physical processes from nature. The link is made explicit in Elliott Carter's Double Concerto, whose fade-out ending was inspired by the closing of Pope's great poem *The Dunciad* – 'Thy hand, great Anarch! lets the curtain fall;/And Universal Darkness buries all.' Here the physical process being metaphorized is nothing less than entropy itself, the winding down of the universe to extinction. The idea of 'dying away to nothing' is inscribed, with pedantic literalness, into the teeming, buzzing incident of the music. The contrast with the easy simplicity, and the fundamental arbitrariness, of a true convention (convention and nature are at opposite poles) could hardly be greater.

What convention (in the old sense) promised, and delivered, was a unity of subjectivity and action. You see that unity in Mozart's scale patterns and cadences, which are both essential elements of the discourse (they are like parts of speech in language, they make the music happen) and expressive. Modernism tore that unity apart, and it is the attempt to bring those two things back together in a new pattern, to conceive of a way of music-making that unites thought and action in a way truly of the present, that I described as forms of 'authenticity'. The attempts to reinstall the old pattern have been described in this chapter. Both are freighted with problems, though the former way seems more honest, and more fruitful.

These two ways of construing the art-music realm now go back a long way. They arose out of the first wave of modernism, and the invasion of the bourgeois musical realm by the popular and the exotic. And they're still an important part of art music today. But after nearly a century, they're losing ground to something wholly new, something that has a better claim to be the music of the new century than anything we've encountered so far.

NOTES

1. Boulez, P. (1976). *Conversations with Célestin Deliège*. London, Eulenberg Books, p. 25.
2. Rosen, C. (2000). *Tradition without Convention: The Impossible Nineteenth-century Project*. The Tanner lectures on Human Values delivered at the University of Utah, 11 April 2000. http://www.tannerlectures.utah.edu/lectures/Rosen_01.pdf

8

✥

The New Naivety

Before we can analyse this new form of music, we have to identify it. And that's difficult, because the peculiar accents of this new 'global music' are everywhere. They can be heard increasingly within the precincts of art music, though they don't arise there; a sign that, finally, art music is giving up the long struggle to keep itself distinct and integral ('pure' if you prefer) and is joining the vast river of the global music industry.

This is itself a sign of the much-vaunted 'breaking down of barriers' which we hear about, a phrase which can be descriptive but is more often hortatory ('we must all work to break down barriers'). We can see this breaking down at the institutional level. Venues which traditionally have been temples of high art now host festivals of pop music alongside symphony orchestras. Funding bodies, both private and public, now

fund musicians like John Zorn who hover somewhere on the border between art and the popular.
Radio stations previously devoted to classical
music are now hospitable to 'avant-rock', and all
those things that come under the capacious term
'left-field'. And as we've seen, at the level of the
music itself, there's no mixing of forms, sounds,
cultures, genres so bizarre and unlikely that
present-day musical culture will not, somewhere,
provide an example of it.

What has survived this incredible melt-down of
distinctions is – ironically enough – a fierce determination to make distinctions. But as we've seen,
the criteria have shifted. John Zorn puts it
succinctly:

> This is something I really react strongly against, the idea
> of high and low art. I mean, that distinction's a bunch of
> fucking bullshit. That's the kind of thing created to make it
> look like you listen to classical music while you're sipping
> champagne and with rock music you're boogeying with
> a bottle of beer and jazz you're in some dirty club with a
> shot of whiskey or some shit like that ... there's good
> music and great music and phoney music in every genre
> and all the genres are the fucking same ... classical music
> is no better than blues because this guy went to school and
> got a degree and studied very cleanly while the other guy
> was out on the street *living* it.[1]

What's striking, apart from the anti-bourgeois
ressentiment, is the way the criterion of quality

becomes the connection with lived experience. This is the kind of 'authenticity' that pop musicians adhere to, and to a degree jazz as well (though jazz musicians often want the other kinds peculiar to classical music, the ones discussed in Chapter 7). Zorn is admirably consistent. The idea of an objective musical realm was and is a creation of the middle class, so if you're going to attack middle-class mores you have to attack the middle-class view of musical value as well.

We've seen what the signs of authenticity can be. In contemporary art music there have been three types: a rage for system, a rage against system, or just plain rage (Zorn falls into the third class). All three are in a way *anti*, forms of music conceived as protests against or rejections of something. But this new form of music, the music that is authentically of *now*, isn't angry about anything. It's soft, it's welcoming. And this is bound to be so, because once you've broken down barriers, once rage has done its work, the stance has to change instantly into its opposite. Instead of strenuous suspicion, universal welcome. Instead of struggle, deep relaxation. In place of rage, a deep, soporific peace.

One of the places you feel its drowsy effects is in the recent wave of enthusiasm for religious-inspired simplicity that has swept the concert hall and CD stores (and again, this is not a phenomenon peculiar to art music, indeed what makes it so peculiarly symptomatic of now is its refusal to obey the art/non-art distinction – or, to put it more strongly and accurately, its determination to break down that distinction). It arose simultaneously during the late 1970s and 1980s in two apparently unconnected musical cultures: Britain and Eastern Europe.

In Britain the chief, indeed only, representative of the trend is John Tavener, a composer who first rose to fame on the back of flower-power (his cantata *The Whale* was released on the Beatles Apple record label). During the late 1960s and 1970s Tavener wrote, among other things, short choral pieces for Anglican usage that show a true composer's instinct for concision and the 'telling moment'. Then came his conversion to a form of Eastern Christian orthodoxy, a conversion which went hand in hand with a rejection: 'I hate progress, I hate development, and I hate evolution in most things; but particularly in music.'[2] (Notice the way Tavener can't escape the modernist condition of being anti.) He had to purge his music of any trace of those things, by returning it to a kind of primal stillness, where sacred texts are sung in long, melismatic lines of a vaguely oriental cast against endlessly sustained drones. In between these long, ululating recitations comes the musical equivalent of ritual actions: gong-strokes, loud brass pedal notes reiterated with solemn slowness, as if a sacred name were being uttered. The music does not grow, develop, or argue with itself; instead it unfolds in vast static friezes, made up of repeating panels of music.

For decades Tavener seemed a marginal figure. But the colossal success of his *Song for Athene*, sung at the funeral of Princess Diana, made it clear that his music touched something in the popular mood. Whatever that mysterious thing was, it wasn't just the ritual inscrutability of the music. Many composers cultivate a sense of ritual distance in their music, indeed it's a keynote of modernist music, which overrides differences in belief and musical style. You find it in composers as different as Olivier Messiaen (where it serves a fervently held Catholic faith) and Harrison Birtwistle, who holds no religious beliefs. But neither of those composers has been plucked to stardom, and the reason isn't hard to find. In Messiaen and Birtwistle the ritual nature of the music doesn't arise from its expressive signs, which are various and complicated. It's to do with something that lies beneath expression, at the level of form. To put it crudely, you could say that the music behaves like a ritual, but it doesn't really sound like one. Birtwistle's *Tragoedia* may be cast in the form of a Greek tragedy, with its stasimons, episodions, etc., but there's absolutely nothing in the music that signals Greekness. Similarly there's nothing in the surface of Messiaen's music that says Catholic.

But you only have to hear a few bars of Tavener's music to pick up a narrow range of easily legible signs, which added together sketch out a world of unfathomable antiquity, fraught with religious import. But – and this is the important thing – notice that the signs are easily consumed precisely because they're not specific. That nasal, undulating vocal line; is it Arabic, Byzantine, Greek? Is it sacred or secular? Is it folky or civilized? The vagueness of reference is deliberate. Tavener doesn't want to compose liturgical music – that would mean abandoning his own creative ego. He confesses to not knowing much about Greek Orthodox 'tones', but he explains that that doesn't matter, because the tones were 'revealed' to the Eastern Church, and his music is also 'revealed' to him rather than being composed in the normal sense. Because of this he can suggest, without a trace of irony, that his music 'harks back to a time before churches and the putting together of liturgies'.[3]

What is notable about Tavener's stance, apart from the egotism, is the way, underneath the orthodox flummery, a kind of debased modernism is still at work. What modernism is deeply uncomfortable with is that form of memory that reveals itself in unconscious, internalized action. Everything must be interrogated, dragged up into the light of consciousness, and then accepted or rejected – normally the latter. In Tavener what is rejected is the Orthodox tradition as handed down and repeated. But the impulse here is not a critical one – it is nothing like Schoenberg's fiercely moralistic rejection of tonality as worn-out and cliché-ridden. What Tavener wants is something that is the very opposite of critical. He wants the enticing image of memory, the image of tradition, without their tiresome constraints. The constraints are bound up with specificity, the rules that say that only *this* chant can be sung on *this* feast-day. To sever the link between memory and action, the specificity of reference must be abolished; thus the deliberate vagueness of the music. This neat rhetorical trick means that Tavener can have his cake and eat it. Tradition is both affirmed and bypassed.

The Estonian composer Arvo Pärt doesn't claim that his brand of religious music was revealed to him by God, which is a blessing. Pärt provides yet another example of a composer whose music suffered a conversion, flipping into its opposite. During the 1960s he wrote a kind of agonizedly dissonant music that is more expressive of spiritual distress than a bold foray into new territory (with good reason: like Górecki and Schnittke and dozens of other aspirant modernists in Eastern Europe and the Soviet Union, Pärt found himself sidelined by the Party-controlled musical institutions of his own country). In the late 1960s, Pärt's mystically inclined Orthodox faith began to show through in the music. In the Third Symphony of 1971 we hear long stretches of simple plainchant, sometimes unadorned, sometimes in plain counterpoint, spiced with a fifteenth-century cadence figure. Like Tavener, Pärt wants to express a religious view of the world that banishes specific historical or traditional references. But his methods are very different. Pärt likes to talk about the way his music expresses and arises out of a primal simplicity, and how the mere playing of single notes very slowly on the piano gives him comfort. But the music gives a rather different image of simplicity, one that is more perceptual than conceptual. In any given piece, every event will be governed by a single process. Contrast, conflict, drama are ruled out of court from the beginning.

Take the *Cantus in Memoriam Benjamin Britten*. We hear unwinding in the high strings a repeated figure, descending from and leaping back to the highest pitch, like a peal of bells. This idealized bell-peal is shadowed at a slightly slower speed, and at a slightly lower pitch. That line is itself shadowed, again at a slower speed, again slightly lower down. By the time the double basses enter, that descending line is shadowed by a myriad versions of itself, the lowest moving with gigantic slowness. The result is a music perpetually quiet, distantly sad, delicately withdrawn, with a sound like layers of gauze moving over one another. And yet this fragile web is produced by a process that unwinds with total mechanistic regularity, like a clockwork toy running down.

Mechanism, regularity, process – does this not sound very modern? Pärt's music recalls Tavener's in its disquieting disjunction between the surface symbols – Christian texts, a vaguely religious stillness – and an underlying modernist sensibility, which asserts its distance from real, lived tradition. But the disjunction in Pärt is more severe, in that the modernist stance goes further. He uses the same constructivist devices which, in a composer of a different temperament, serve a grotesquely parodic intent. Take the piece *Tabula Rasa* for string orchestra and prepared piano. Again the orchestra is treated like a gigantic array of cogs and wheels, which turn with iron inevitability. One of those cogs is projected by the double basses, which play a simple repeating up-and-down scale. On each repetition, the scale increases in ambit, ascending one step higher, and descending one step lower. There comes a point where the descending portion of the scale reaches down to a point below the bottom end of the double-basses' range. The logic of the process runs up against the limit of the instrument, at which point the double basses simply stop playing.

This idea could be comic. It certainly has a grim humour at the beginning of the Piano Concerto by the Hungarian composer György Ligeti, where we hear a dancing figure ascend so high up the piano keyboard that it 'disappears' off the end, only to reappear at the bottom end. The idea is given an extra twist in several pieces by that cheerfully anarchic Irish composer Gerald Barry. In his orchestral piece *Flamboys* a melody lifted from his earlier piece *Bob* is reused, but transposed way down into the bass region – so low, in fact, that some of the notes lie beyond the range of the instruments. Barry simply omits them, so the melody gains a curious new 'gapped' quality.

This example is a reminder of a very important fact about modernist music, which is that its procedures and material are not bound up with any particular expressive quality. Which is why Pärt can seize hold of the mechanistic strain in modern music, and turn it to the purposes of a tranced, ecstatic stillness. In this respect, modernist music is the true heir of 'classical music', whose material is also expressively neutral. An appoggiatura can be graceful, or it can be yearning. A fugue can be doleful, or sprightly, or tragic. A perfect cadence expresses nothing – that is why it is so useful.

This points to the deep chasm between these two composers, too often lumped together as representatives of 'holy minimalism'. For a while it seemed as though Pärt might have travelled the same path as Tavener. In the 1960s there was an overt use of musical means expressive of holiness and antiquity; plainchant, movement in parallel fifths. But his mature music, from the mid-1970s onwards, shows an awareness that this will not do. Either one chooses the path of tradition, or one forswears it entirely, in order to find some truly contemporary means whereby those attributes of the sacred – stillness, unity, concord – can be expressed.

The idea that modernism could be turned against itself goes a long way back, back in fact to the period around World War I. In Yeats's automatic writing, in Kandinsky's writings on art, in the music of that group of Russian mystical composers like Obukhov and Skryabin, one sees an attempt to subvert convention and tradition as fierce as the more overtly 'modern' innovators. But the aim is not to usher in a specifically modern world-view; it's more an attempt to restore a primal unity of affect and action, of inner and outer; the unity that obtained before the apparatus of culture – conventions, traditions and institutions – laid its deadening influence on the world. Unsurprisingly, the latent mystical strain in modernism took vigorous root in the USA, where it joined hands with a suspicion of the decadent ways of the Old World. During the 1940s and 1950s it led that rugged pioneer Harry Partch to create a whole orchestra of new instruments, designed to restore the ancient purities of Pythagorean tuning. The idea of returning to ancient wisdom enjoyed a massive upsurge with the counter-culture of the 1960s. LaMonte

Young's Theater of Eternal Music set out to revive the latent power of pure intervals, creating vast pieces that were little more than decorated drones played at deafening volume.

Simplicity is the hallmark of this music. But as a descriptive term applied to artworks, the word 'simple' is far from simple. Simplicity can be the result of a culture at its height, rather than the rejection of culture (as it is in, say, Mozart's *Magic Flute*, or the last pages of Beethoven's last string quartet). And as the example of Pärt shows, there is a distinction between simplicity as a structural principle and as a perceptual result. His *Cantus in Memoriam Benjamin Britten* may be simple in concept, but the concept produces a tangle of lines which is hard for the ear to unravel. And even where the music really is simple in its audible features, the expressive import of those features may be anything but. Minimalism may be taken as a demonstration *ad absurdum* of that truth.

Things get even more complicated with a composer like György Kurtág, Ligeti's rival for the title of greatest living Hungarian composer. His music is often ascetically bare in texture, made up of tiny, wispy melodic and harmonic fragments surrounded by silence. So beautifully fashioned and weighed are these fragments that they take on an immense significance. The idea that poverty is a kind of riches is a familiar one in painting, as witnessed by, among others, the Arte Povera group of the 1950s. It's a common theme in music too, though only in Kurtág, and in one or two other composers like the Italian Giacinto Scelsi, does it have that sense of asceticism, as if the musical substance itself has become rags and patches. More often it's a conceptual idea of 'paring down to essentials', in which case a more appropriate painterly comparison would be Abstract Expressionism. Mark Rothko in particular is a hero figure for many composers, including Gerald Barry and the South African composer Kevin Volans. Volans' String Quartet no.6 combines minimalist concentration of means with a floating, tranced quality that is worlds away from the driving energy of a Reich or Glass.

All this is by way of preamble and contrast to the specifically new form of 'simplicity', of which we've already had a taste in Tavener. This new sort avoids any hi-falutin' appeal to Pythagorean tuning systems. It does not clothe itself in rags and patches – on the contrary it often has a de luxe richness of sound. It does not embrace system and process. It doesn't even have to be religious in tone. What is does is to take the familiar expressive means of Western classical music, and bathe them in a kind of forgetfulness. This lends these familiar things a kind of innocence, and a strange kind of pallor.

A good illustration of both the innocence and the pallor can be found in the piece that was the

classical hit of 1993. That was the year Henryk
Górecki's Third Symphony was released on CD
for the first time, and it catapulted this obscure
Polish composer to fame. His story is not unlike
Pärt's. Up to the 1960s he wrote music in a crash-
ingly dissonant style, burdened with anxiety and
distress, which gained him a certain cachet in the
West. But by the early 1970s a new simplicity
was starting to emerge in the music, whose source
can be seen in titles like 'Old Polish Music'
(though it would be many years before the folk
element became audible in the music). In the Third
Symphony all trace of dissonance was banished,
to the astonishment and dismay of its first audience at the Warsaw Festival in 1976 (this was a
rare if not unique outpost of *avant-gardism* in
Eastern Europe).

The symphony is a fascinating piece, because
it's poised right on the cusp of 'old new music' and
'new new music'. The monomania, the refusal
of the music to modulate itself in the light of its
own developing experience, is quintessentially
old-modern. The new aspect of the music is the
way it evokes the expressive power of tonality
while avoiding its psychological dynamic. We see
the latter tendency unequivocally displayed in the
second movement. It's a setting of a message of
comfort from a Jewish prisoner of the Gestapo
to his mother, which he scratched on to the wall of
his cell. The first few bars of the movement could

be a motto of the way new music is now; it could, if you like, be the theme tune of 'new century music'. What we hear is a simple, plangent three-note melodic phrase outlining a simple harmonic change, a change that in the old days of the common practice would have been labelled I^7 to IVc. But the salient notes of the first harmony hang over into the second, creating a blurring effect. It lends the phrase a kind of hopeless sadness, and also a kind of passivity (the one is linked to the other; the passive attitude kills hope).

Why should this little phrase be so significant? Because it shows how the tonality one finds in 'new-new' music is profoundly different to the sort that governed music until the end of the nineteenth century; so different, in fact, that it really ought not to bear the same name. The idea of a 'return to tonality' is inherently contradictory anyway, because it suggests that tonality is the natural musical voice of mankind, waiting to reclaim its inheritance once the brief madness of modernism was over. This is the view of latter-day romantics like Robin Holloway, who was once photographed in a T-shirt bearing the legend 'tonality lives!' But tonality, as we've seen, can't be seen as a pure voice of nature, however much it may be rooted in acoustics. It is also a histori-cally determined phenomenon. In its forward movement, its precarious balancing of outward exploration and homecoming, it is the perfect expression of a form of subjectivity that came into being and flourished during the eighteenth and nineteenth centuries. As we're always being assured by post-modern theorists, that form of subjectivity no longer exists (though the memory of it is comforting, which is one reason why old forms of classical music keep their appeal). So it must be the case that the new tonality works in a very different way, and that its similarities to the old way may be only superficial.

This may seem a surprising assertion, because on the face of it the similarities between new tonality and the old sort are overwhelming. So much new tonal music seems like a pastiche, or parody, of old tonal music. In Robin Holloway's Serenade in G the evocation of the opulent harmonic palette of Richard Strauss's late works is so good that it sounds like the real thing; too much like it, in fact, to make for a comfortable listening experience. There's a similar unease with the Schumann-imitations one encounters in George Rochberg's music. It's hard to say whether the sense of something being not quite right lies in the music itself (in the sense that the parody is not as perfect as it seemed to be at first) or the sense of historical dislocation it brings. But those things are bound to be difficult to disentangle. A genuine tonal language – despite the efforts of the conservatoires and the writers of composition manuals – cannot be described in a purely formal, ahistorical way, unless one is content to write pastiche. It contains an ineradicable historical element.

During the period of common practice, that historical element was in a sense invisible. It really did seem as if tonality was one, indivisible thing, a network of relationships in which Wagner's chromaticism and Bach's chromaticism could be seen as permanent existing possibilities. For us this is no longer true. Tonality in contemporary art music is not the continuation of the old common practice; it is a critique, or a parody, or pastiche of that practice. Every feature of the new tonality is marked by a distance, or even a parodic inversion, of its model.

That distance is often ironic, but in the case of Holloway or Rochberg, the distance is hardly ironic; it is a straightforward desire to re-enter a lost paradise. Desire is indeed the engine of the new tonality. Composers want that ready link with expressivity, and the connection with the desires of the audience, that tonality gives. But desire is often mixed with other things – resentment, or a determination to show that, though one wants the power of tonality, one isn't going to be bound by its protocols. You find this in John Adams, where those forms of tonality useful for creating a sense of forward-driving climax are invoked only when he wants them – they don't govern the discourse. Again, the second movement of his *El Dorado* provides a *locus classicus* of the new tonality. At first, there's a static alternation of added sixth and seventh 'road-movie' harmonies whose link to tonal practice is so tenuous as to be non-existent. But then, when the music swells to its climax, Adams brings in harmonic progressions, which can be spelt out in old root-governed nomenclature. The latent dynamism of that minimalist tick receives, so to speak, the imprimatur of tradition.

The danger with Adams's method is that it creates a fundamental duality in the discourse. But such is Adams' skill that he persuades you that oil and water really can mix. The unity of an Adams piece is entirely at the level of rhetoric and motor rhythm (that minimalist tick), which together are remarkably effective at papering over the cracks. Philip Glass's music is much more of a genuine unity. In his recent music the harmonic language has been purged of its earlier ambiguity and is now made up entirely of the simplest elements – triads, seventh chords, added sixths. In his Fifth Symphony they give an effect of wide-eyed innocence, fully in keeping with the symphony's message, which is that, at bottom, all religions enunciate the same truths. The innocence, though, is not just to do with the choice of elements; it's just as much a result of the logic that binds them together.

To see how that logic works, we need to glance back at the old one. In a piece of 'old' tonal music, it's very hard to tell whether the chords arise as a result of lines intersecting, or whether the procession of chords is primary, with the lines then strung between them like garlands. This obvious fact shows that harmony and counterpoint are really the same thing, and that one or the other will jump into prominence according to whether music is being viewed from the 'vertical' or 'horizontal' perspective. In the new tonality, these two things fall apart. Chords and lines tend to assert their own planes of existence, which remain stubbornly separate. The independence is bound to show itself as incompetence, because technical competence in harmony and counterpoint is precisely to do with making it seem as if line and chord belong together as naturally as a body and its shadow. At a certain point in the first movement of Glass's Fifth Symphony, a repeated chordal sequence is overlaid with scale patterns. One imagines that the patterns will lend their weight to the sequence, so that the two arrive at a meeting point with what seems like 'logical' inevitability. In fact the scale patterns have to be interrupted and 'tweaked' in their ascent, to make them agree with the unfolding chordal pattern below. The effect is to banish, in an instant, any sense of logic in the old sense. In Glass's live performances there are much more egregiously 'wrong' moments when a simple dominant-tonic movement in the keyboards is contradicted by a melody line, which stays firmly in the dominant.

This quirk is not peculiar to Glass. One finds it often in the music of Michael Nyman, though in his case the expressive effect is more complicated. In the case of Glass, the bleached out stasis of the music makes it easy to read incompetence as innocence. In Nyman's music, it's more unsettling, because we're assailed by all the marks of emotional intensity: hammered chords, surging melody lines, often doubled in octaves, and a frequent use of that ancient signal of expressivity, a dissonant melody note which 'sighs' downwards to a consonant one. In his score to the film *The Commissar Vanishes* (Nyman, like Glass, is at his best when writing for the movies) there's a moment when the music suggests a gesture of closure that was conventional in the fifteenth and sixteenth centuries. But while one part moves as it should, another refuses to budge. Nyman treats the old technique as if it were a picturesque ruin, imitating certain aspects of it without appearing to understand its original meaning.

It's only in post-minimalist composers like Glass and Nyman that these things take on the aspect of grammatical solecisms. Without that insistent beat, which inculcates an expectation of grammatical propriety (in music, grammar is all to do with delineating and, so to speak, legitimizing a forward motion) the mismatch of line and chord leans more towards pathos. We've already seen one example of that, in Górecki. It's a common feature of Eastern European music, where this 'new tonality' seems to be even more widespread (the fact that this trend can take root in such disparate cultures is a sign of its massive importance). Valentine Silvestrov's *Post-scriptum* is typical of his *faux-naif* way of moving harmonies up and down by step – the method of children making their first steps at harmonizing a melody at the piano.

The neutering of voice-leading and part-writing is one way of avoiding the dynamic, directional implications of old tonality. Another way is to install a circular movement in place of a directional one. New tonal music of the last two decades affords hundreds if not thousands of examples of such circular movements, in the form of short chordal patterns which repeat endlessly. Glass's music relies on them totally. The first movement of his Fifth Symphony has a good example at about the half-way point – good in the sense that it has a certain piquancy, and is five harmonies in length, a pleasant change from the normal use of two- and four-length units. The piquancy arises from the way each harmony is derived from the previous one by shifting the elements a whole or half-step. This invokes the old power of part-writing; it suggests, if only faintly, that what we have here is a real play of lines, which yields, as if by magic, an array of harmonies.

One great advantage of using these repeating patterns is that they bring a portion of classical music back within the orbit of the popular. Until recently, art music's attitude to popular music has been like that of the English country squire who invites the yokels in once a year for a glass of small beer, and the rest of the year ignores them. This *de haut en bas* attitude showed itself as early as the 1890s, when café-concert idioms started to appear in art music, followed, a decade or two later, by the cakewalk and ragtime. There was a kind of aesthetic congruence between jazz and the neo-classical strain in modern music, which meant that the jazz pieces of Stravinsky, Milhaud, Copland *et al.* had a certain internal consistency. In the music of post-World War II modernist composers, the encounter with the popular was bound to be less happy, precisely because the 'second wave' of modernism was hostile through and through to the popular. However after the thawing and loosening of modernism in the 1960s, some composers felt that a *frisson* of the street would be just the thing, and an electric guitar would appear in the score. The results were, in nearly every case, toe-curlingly awful, with the piece sounding hopelessly dated the moment it was unveiled.

But by then the traffic was no longer one-way. Pop music was beginning to feel that it had a claim to the high ground (a claim made some decades earlier by jazz). During the 1970s and 1980s Village Voice promoted the art credentials of pop and rock; for example Gregory Sandow described Glenn Branca's music as 'classical music for loud guitars'.[4] At around the same time Rhys Chatham worked with overtones, a formal preoccupation which made him a slight misfit in a rock milieu, despite his avowed attraction to its sex and violence. Chatham actually described himself as a 'not-not-rocker', a term which presages the currently trendy term 'un-pop'.[5]

If pop music has its 'un-pop' side, classical music has its 'un-classical' side, peopled by composers and performers who come out of a classical milieu but are bored by its formalities, envious of pop's vast popular appeal, and angry with what they see as the cerebral sterility of modernist music (though they have a hankering for its intellectual cachet). What these composers create is not pop music; it's for listening, not dancing, to and it uses acoustic forces, and extended forms, which belong in the concert hall. Nevertheless, their music does share a real, deep-seated formal feature with pop music, which is the omnipresence of repeating harmonic patterns. An example from pop which is typical in its four-unit pattern is Dylan's 'Lay lady lay', though its interesting combination of a bass pattern (two ascending major thirds, linked by a descending tritone) and a descending semitonal line in the treble makes it stand out from the crowd. These patterns – of which soul in particular affords thousands of examples – tend to be non-functional, that's to say, not impelled by root progressions or real voice-leading. The louche, laid-back atmosphere this engenders is abetted by the chords themselves, which avoid the sharpened seventh (the sharpened seventh, or 'leading note' is, as its name implies, an indispensable element in the dynamic impetus of tonality). The repetition of the sequence teaches us to hear it as somehow meant; rhetoric takes the place of grammar (underneath the slouching body-language, there is the method of the demagogue). The music says 'be seduced by the noise these chords make, don't worry that they don't follow'. We're willing to be seduced because the chords are euphonious in themselves, and there are, here and there, echoes of older, rule-bound practice (4–3 suspensions are common, but the harmonic linkage never extends beyond two chords). Grammar is entirely subservient to appetite. We hear a similar subservience in Glass's Fifth Symphony, though there the elements in the repeating pattern have a more classical feel.

There is another form of repetition, found in both hip-hop and certain areas of art music, where even the bare requirement of euphony is dispensed with. Here the repeating units, or 'licks' as they are called in hip-hop, are much shorter, short enough for them to be the vehicle of the music's aggressively insistent rhythmic idiom. Because the mere fact of 4 × 4 regularity is a sufficient defining feature, anything can function as a 'lick', even a fragment of a Schoenberg tone-row.[6] Once that is established, literally anything can be flung against it: sampled noises, speech, fragments of tonal music, whatever. The technique has now worked its way into areas of art music. The power of the lick is dramatized in *Amelia, Flying*, a piece jointly composed by the three leading lights in the New York-based group Bang on a Can Allstars. At the beginning the music makes a brief but strenuous attempt to dislodge the massive harmonic and rhythmic stability of the lick, which here consists of just two notes, E and G. The attempt fails, but it is renewed at much greater length towards the end. The vestigial drama this scheme outlines is what ties the piece to the art sphere; to appreciate it, you have to pay attention all the way through. But in its sound, its technology, its evocation of the 'social body' (in this case a distinctly sweaty one) the piece owes much to a pop sensibility.

This kind of collage technique, where vastly disparate sounds and references are ruled with a rod of iron by a 'lick', would not be possible without digital samplers. The sampler, which records sounds in digital form and then reproduces them at different pitches, exemplifies the way digital technology has blurred or even abolished the distinction between production and reproduction. At one time this distinction seemed as natural and immovable a part of the musical landscape as the distinction between wind and stringed instruments. On the one hand, you had reproductive devices – record players, radios, tape recorders – and on the other, productive devices: synthesizers, oscillators, and 'instruments' like the Ondes Martenot. The advent of the tape recorder started to blur the distinction, as it could be used to make sounds as well as record them. But the sampler is different, because it swallows up the previously distinct realm of sound synthesis. A sample of a digital synthesizer note is the same, physically speaking, as the original; it is a bundle of information. This means that to import sounds from many disparate sources into one musical statement can be done easily and inexpensively. It was a trend first seen in pop music. Hip-hoppers like Bomb the Bass reproduced entire licks from James Brown songs, while John Oswald's 'plunderphonics' made use of entire songs. But in the last decade composers within art music have started to plunder the world's musics for evocative sounds. Jocelyn Pook, famous for the sound-track she composed for Stanley Kubrick's last film *Eyes Wide Shut*, roams both outwards and back in time for her sources. Her *Blow the Wind Southerly: Piè*

Jesu uses Kathleen Ferrier's famous recording of 'Blow the Wind Southerly', while *Red Song* mixes string sounds with samples of Verdi's Requiem and Tartar folk song. The sources are mixed with live performance, as they are in the Kronos Quartet's recent album *Nuevo*, where the quartet's sounds are mixed with street sounds from Mexico, crying children, and the strange high-pitched squeak of the musical leaf, all recorded *in situ* in Central America.

> To learn by heart is to afford the text or music an indwelling clarity and life-force ... the archaic Greek belief that memory is the mother of the Muses expresses a fundamental insight into the nature of the arts and the mind.[7]

One word has been gradually pushing itself forward over the course of this chapter: evocation. Evocation – of other places, other times, other cultures – is what music is becoming increasingly devoted to. It's a symptom of a deep change in the way memory functions in music. For a traditional musician, memory is what is revealed in action. The store of learnt melodies is not possessed in some abstract sense; he could not write them down. This is why the melodies change over the centuries, because memory prescribes a set of actions rather than a fixed image, and a set of actions can never be repeated exactly.

In classical music of the common practice, things are less clear-cut. Rapid changes in the tonal language mean that the passage from stored-up memory to action is not quite so smooth. The surface complication of the music has to be reduced to a set of grammatical procedures, which don't quite capture the complexity of the reality they purport to describe. But the grammatical unity underlying the music does at least allow a new sort of memory to spring forth, one best described by the word allusion. Pieces within the common practice are all caught in this web of allusion, which works both forwards and backwards; Mozart can, at times, allude to Wagner, and vice versa. It is this web of cross-reference which gives music of the tonal period its peculiar power. Allusion is a substitute, for the listener, of the active unity possessed by the performer.

Allusion worked its magic at least up to the early works of Schoenberg and Stravinsky, and in the case of Stravinsky into his neo-classical works of the pre-war period as well. But with the postwar modernists, the web falls apart. (Or perhaps it would be more accurate to say it was torn down in a fit of pique. Destroying memory was part of the avant-garde project.) Now, in the music of new tonal composers, and in the music of cross-over performers and composers, memory is back with a vengeance. But it works in a completely different way. The old form of allusive memory went hand in hand with an expressive conception of music.

To function properly, it required a perceptible unity both at the level of the individual piece, and the tradition (thus the 'web of allusion' referred to above). It needed it because expressivity implies the presence of an agent, a something or somebody that is doing the expressing.

But the striking thing about many examples of new tonal music is precisely their *dis*unity. The expressive elements are taken from different periods, different cultures, with the result that the music itself becomes hard to read as issuing from a single ordering subjectivity. This accounts for the peculiar chilliness of music that dwells in this ambient/crossover/fusion territory. Warmth only attaches to an expressive gesture when we can conceive of it as issuing from the same guiding hand as the previous gesture, and the one after. The music of computer composer Paul Lansky often mixes tonal chords in with the disjointed speech patterns, or traffic noises, which constitute the real substance of the music. But the two don't link up with each other. What holds the discourse together is the floating electronic ambience, which engorges everything and anything with the same indifference. And when, as often happens, the sampled sounds of the everyday world fall into a repetitive pattern, we get a new kind of unity: a purely mechanical unity of beat, which unifies the music's disparate sources in the same way as the clattering wheels of a subway train lend, at an unconscious level, a sense of 'unity' to the passengers.

The word 'unconscious' is another important one in this context. When musical discourse is a real, lived unity, the question of its unconscious side cannot arise. Even if all of the tradition cannot be literally present in the mind or the fingers at once, it is all there *in potentia*, ready to be called forth by the appropriate stimulus or occasion. But when musical discourse is made up of evocations which have no grammatical or cultural connection with each other, large parts of it are bound to fall into an unconscious state. This curious fact is revealed in the expressive colour of much 'cross-over' music, which seems to exist in a perpetual dream. Notice also that when things are pushed into an unconscious realm they suffer a kind of levelling. The distinction between a genuine recalled memory, and an evocation of something contemporary, but distant in a different way, simply vanishes. The examples given above from Jocelyn Pook illustrate the point nicely. Kathleen Ferrier's marvellous recording of 'Blow the Wind Southerly' will be a real memory (a precious one too) for many music-lovers in Britain, and quite a few beyond it as well. The sampled Tartar singing on *Red Song* of course won't be. But in Pook's music both these things take on the same expressive flavour of something strangely familiar and yet unfamiliar, an irruption of the dream-world into the everyday.

This unconscious aspect of the discourse has a profound effect on its grammar, the way things are prepared, led up to, and departed from. One of the things that gives figures in a dream their dream-like character is the utterly arbitrary nature of their coming and going. They simply appear and disappear. So it is with the elements in all those forms of music where new technology has a role. The bit of gear that facilitates this appearing and disappearing is not new; it's the fader, a familiar item in studios since the advent of multi-track tape recorders in the 1960s. The fader and the sampler are the twin pillars of today's musical world. You hear their potent double-act in an album like Nitin Sawnhey's *Prophecy*, which gets its dreaminess precisely from the power of the fader to change the colour and weight of the sampled elements bit by bit. There are no real events, no sharp edges. Here the elements are heterogeneous; bits of a political speech, temple chanting, synthesized drones, a shakuhachi. But the same technique can be applied to elements which apparently all refer to the same source, in which case the effect is even odder, as if the members of a close-knit family were suddenly unable to understand one another. You hear it in the aptly named track *Frozen* from the album *NP3* by Norwegian jazz trumpeter Nils Petter Molvaer, where the elements evoke an off-the-peg romanticism; ponderous minor-mode melodies, lots of Lisztian pianistic flourishes. Notice how the arrival and departure of elements is managed not by any of the old grammatical devices – form, development, counterpoint, and so on – but simply by pushing a fader up or down.

It could be objected that this CD shouldn't even feature in a book devoted to art music. But who these days can say with confidence what belongs to serious music, and what doesn't? If 'truth to the times' is one criterion of seriousness, then Molvaer could be said to be more serious than Pierre Boulez, whose music breathes the air of a bygone era. And if institutional approbation is any guide, then this music must be serious, as I encountered it on the BBC's classical music station. Despite all that, it seems to me not merely a bad piece of music, but a pernicious one. And in the last chapter I shall try to say why, despite all the blurring of boundaries, judgement is still possible and necessary.

NOTES

1. John Zorn, interview with Edward Strickland, February 1988, quoted in http://www.ddjackson.com/th_quot.html
2. Tavener, J. (2000). *The Music of Silence: A Composer's Testament*, ed. Brian Keble. London, Faber & Faber, p. 14.
3. *Ibid.*, p. 134.

4. From Paul Theberge: 'Random Access: Music, Technology, Postmodernism', in Simon Miller (ed.) (1993). *The Last Post: Music after Post-modernism*. Manchester, Manchester University Press.

5. See for example Neil Currie's essay on 'unpop' at www. demon.co.uk/momus/thought061000.html

6. Personal communication from Kyung Sun Min.

7. Steiner, G. (1989). *Real Presences*. London, Faber & Faber, p. 9.

9

❧

Rediscovering Music

In the vast, booming, buzzing confusion that is music today, classical music is a backwater. In terms of CD sales, it is around 8 per cent of the market in the West and Japan, and much less elsewhere. And what audience there is in the concert hall is greying, and therefore shrinking. Younger people are happy to listen to classical music on the radio, but they don't buy CDs or concert tickets,[1] so their interest is of no help in maintaining classical music as a living art. Within classical music, the audience for new music is itself a minority.

The precarious position of art music within the marketplace might not matter so much if its accustomed high place in the priorities of the Western world's cultural ministries, cultural foundations and educational systems were assured. But it is not. Everywhere in the Western world, classical music is losing ground to other forms of music in terms of state funding. Classical music's problem is that it cannot plead its case, because it finds itself caught in a double bind. Its universal aspirations means it has no appeal to the new politics of identity, which is now leading funding priorities in the arts. Forms of music are these days valued for the way they legitimate and express feelings of group belonging. But neither can classical music appeal to 'inclusivity', the other great mantra of arts funding. To be counted as inclusive these days an art form must appeal to literally everybody – an absurd demand that is impossible for any cultural form to meet, high or low. Like any other cultural form, classical music only appeals to those prepared to meet it half-way by learning its forms, its vocabulary. But in classical music this universal fact about cultural forms is perceived as specially problematic. To counteract it an orchestra these days has to be a social chameleon, dressing up in trainers and baseball caps for the children's concert and education events, than bathing itself in purple light for the chill-out classical concert, then quickly donning tie and tails for the sponsors' reception and the formal evening concert. The result has been a continuing identity crisis, and a debilitating sense of anxiety among classical musicians and managers, a sense that they must always be justifying their existence.

However, the trend towards the 'hyper-demo-cratizing' of classical music, to borrow George Walden's term,[2] hardly originates with Arts Councils and Cultural Departments. It is the latest chapter in the long story of the changing nature of music, from something participated in, to something merely consumed. As we've seen, classical music arises at an ambiguous moment in that process, a moment where participation changes its meaning. Instead of being a sign of music's social function, participation – by both performer and listener – is the investment that wrests music *away* from its social function, to constitute an autonomous realm (of course music continues to be a social event, but it is one sustained and, so to speak, legitimated by an idea of music's autonomy). On the performer's side, the realm is the inherited body of rules, turns of phrase, conventions, expressed through performative or composing skill. On the listener's side, it is those very same things, called into being through active, strenuous engagement with the music being performed.

That engagement was bolstered by two things: repeated acquaintance with the music, and participation in the form of amateur performance. It cannot be stressed too often that active listening feeds on participation. If the Victorians seem to have had better concentration than us, it's only because their engagement as listeners was felt in the fingers and body as much as processed in the mind. And they had less music to focus on, as the concert hall and sheet music was their only source of music. The information overload brought on by radio, CD and the internet had not yet arrived; plus there were domestic servants to look after the chores. They were able to give music the thing it needs most: time.

We have very little time, and so much music to consume – which is why expressiveness in music is these days shrinking to a purely adjectival form. A century ago, when participation already was giving way to listening, words about music were becoming extraordinarily important. But the use of words was part of an unspoken pact in which the listener acknowledged the inadequacy of words, even while making use of them (in the form of programme notes, primers on music, etc.). That pact has now dissolved, and the symptom of this dissolving is the shrinkage of the modes in which words relate to music. I don't mean to suggest that good writing on music can no longer be found. But what sets the tone of writing about music these days is not the elegantly written critical tome or programme note or review. It is the telegraphic descriptions, previews and summary judgements that swarm through magazines and PR brochures and newspaper supplements, and across the internet. Instead of *explanation of* music, or interpretation of it, what these give us is something much more amenable to readers in a hurry – a kind of portmanteau description which annuls the distance between itself and the music (a distance which the old descriptions were keen to preserve, even as they embraced description). What this amounts to is a takeover of music by words. Words are quick and easy; music is slow, it takes its own time, and its meaning is slippery and difficult.

The oft-heard complaint about new music, that there are plenty of good composers but no really startlingly original voices, is as much a product of this verbal veil as it is of the music itself. What the system of previewing, PR, commentary, etc. requires is music that offers itself up for quick description; the unprecedented, which the system claims always to be in search of, is at bottom unwelcome, because by definition it eludes description. This fact, rather than any dearth of original talent, is why we're surrounded by so much music that sounds *like* something else, but not very much like itself. The 'new' new music that flourishes on the borders of the old genres – chill-out classical, sampledelia, all the numberless varieties of fusion musics – actually turns what used to be a subsidiary aspect of music into a *raison d'être*. This is the power of music to evoke things. We're surrounded these days by quickly digestible evocative elements: a quick burst of shakuhachi (signifying the quaintness of old Japan) here, a sudden surge of strings (signifying 'warmth') there.

The rise in evocativeness goes hand in hand with an ebbing away of interest in the unadorned musical event. There's a growing sense that music on its own is inadequate, which manifests itself in the calls to make classical concerts more visually appealing, and in the current vogue for multi-media events. In the early twenty-first century, we seem to be going back to the aesthetic of the Baroque, when music was thought to be powerless unless conjoined to words or images.[3] That trend also lies behind the galloping convergence of classical music and film music. Cast your eye down the list of classical best-selling CDs in any given month and you're sure to find a couple of film score CDs among the top ten, and any orchestral season nowadays includes at least one 'Night at the Movies'.

When music is taken over by words, it loses its identity as music. It becomes simply another item in the world's consumerist furniture, an item which just happens to work through the ear rather than the eye or the skin. The entire *raison d'être* of modern music was to resist that takeover, by preserving the integrity of the 'musical realm'. But the alarming thing about so much new music that claims to be serious is that it connives at that takeover. It's 'stuff' barely constitutes anything like a realm, so captive is it to expressivity. And working in tandem with this linguistic tendency to sub-jectivity are vast social forces pushing all music towards a solitary mode of experience.

This transforming of music, in our time, from a social experience to a solitary one was already prefigured in the nineteenth century (remember Nietzsche on the private nature of the experience of Wagner). But it's only in recent years that the technology to make music a literally private experience has become available. The record player and radio reduced the musical space from something communal to something family-sized, namely the living-room. Now, thanks to the Walkman, it's reduced even further, to the space between one's ears. The Walkman, even more than the sampler and the mixer, is the great symbolic musical technology of our time, because it so perfectly symbolizes the parodic inversion of music's being. At one time a necessarily social activity, which enlarged the individual through co-ordinated action and experience, music has now become the means by which we hold our fellow humans at bay. When you wear a Walk-man, you're saying to the world, don't bug me. There's another parodic inversion performed by the Walkman, this time on the notion of music's autonomy and 'portability'. This, remember, was that peculiar ability of art music to move from one social space to another. To make that move, a piece of music had to change its aural dress; a dance might become a lute piece. But underneath the changed surface, an identity persisted. This inculcated the idea that beneath or above social function, and beneath surface appearances, there was a 'purely musical' realm, one that came to be known as classical music.

But when music emerges from the speakers of a Walkman, it no longer exists 'in itself'. It exists 'for us', summoned into being only when it suits our needs, resounding in our heads alone. And when that happens, the autonomy of the 'musical realm' vanishes, as it's no longer needed. The irony is that this fate was lying in wait for music the moment it became 'autonomous', because as Terry Eagleton points out, autonomy is a double-edged thing:

> When art becomes a commodity, it is released from its traditional functions within church, court and state into the autonomous freedom of the market place. Now it exists, not for any specific audience, but just for anybody with the taste to appreciate it and the money to buy it. And in so far as it exists for nothing and nobody in particular, it can be said to exist for itself. It is 'independent' because it has been swallowed up by commodity production.[4]

Caught between these two massive forces – a consumerist aesthetic which wants to reduce music to a consumable sign, and a cultural climate hostile to anything that smacks of elitism – it's a wonder anything more challenging than Tavener and Pook survives at all. And yet modernism does survive, and even flourishes. The astonishing thing is how many 20- or 30-something composers choose to express themselves in a modernist idiom, when all the career pressures are to become a John Adams clone, or write film music. Why should this be, when the problems that have always attended modernist music – above all its tendency to empty concert halls – are now exacerbated by official disfavour?

One answer to that is given by the composer Robin Holloway in his essay 'Modernism and After'.[5] He claims that these days modernism has now itself become another form of nostalgia, no different in kind to the nostalgia that leads him and other neo-tonal composers to recreate the romanticism of Schumann, or the numerous other kinds of music that seek to go back. Young composers like Johannes Maria Staud, or Luke Stoneham, or Simon Holt, on this view have simply been seduced by the glamour of the modernist stance of perpetual revolution, the heroic artist holding out for artistic truth against the purblind laziness of the public. But as Holloway himself says in the same essay, 'nostalgia is a burning emotion, fierce rather than enervating, purposeful rather than lazy'.[6] Indeed: which is why, rather than dismissing the young modernists as pale epigones of a movement that's lost its force, it might be better to see them as evidence that the modernist stance is still as necessary, still as symptomatic of the defining problem of contemporary musical culture, as it was in 1910 and 1950.

That problem hasn't been changed by the new technologies of sound production and reproduction, it's simply been wound up to fever-pitch. It is the problem that faces art music when its formal means can no longer cope with the multiplicity of its substance. When that happens, the musical realm loses its integrity. It is that loss of unity which brings about nostalgia, which above all is a yearning for wholeness. As the new fusion music shows, that wholeness cannot be engendered, or even suggested, by a style that merely pillages from the past, or from exotic sources. The sources remain stubbornly separate, glued together merely at the pre-conscious level by devices like the drone, and that dreamy ambience of the ambient/ fusion soundworld.

Faced with the evident banality of much of this music, the response of a 'classical' composer in search of a real, active unity in music – one that restores music to a full consciousness and which banishes dreaminess – is always to feel that the solution lies in the composing process. If only the act of co-ordinating the compositional process with the dizzying multiplicity of available sources could be got right, then order would be restored, and that fierce burning nostalgia would melt into true happiness. That in the end is what both the new tonal composers (or at least those with a conscience, like Holloway) and the modernists are both searching for: a form of musical discourse that unites memory, experience and action in a perceptible, lived unity.

But the idea that it lies within the power of composers to bring about that happy state is simply to reinstall the problem that led to the modernist break in the first place. Left to their own devices, composers (whether conservative or radical) tend to come up with grand schemes – 'the serial revolution', 'back to tonality' – whose connection with the real world of music-making is tenuous, to say the least. The reason for this is that composers tend not to interrogate the unspoken assumption of their art, which is that its substance is ideal, floating above history. This is why Holloway is able to suggest, in all seriousness, that composers should look at the vast field of classical music (and indeed other musics) and tease out the possibilities in the material that failed to emerge when those styles were current. 'History and hindsight', he says, 'tend to make factitious inevitability out of what must in fact have been completely fluid. The choices made, the paths taken, were not the only possibilities ... the past is full of paths not taken, branches that didn't flower, latent and nascent alternatives that a composer can return to, develop and bring into being "what might have been".'[7]

Is Holloway really suggesting that the coincidence of Beethoven's driving, sharply polarized tonality and that vast upheaval in consciousness brought on by the French Revolution is 'purely factitious'? Or that the sudden upsurge in exotic musical vocabulary in the late nineteenth century is utterly unconnected with the imperial adventures of the European powers? The idea that the choice of musical forms and vocabularies could be entirely free of history seems implausible at the outset. But let's imagine a musical culture where composers took Holloway's advice. What would determine which of these many paths the composer might take? Presumably, his or her whim, the constraining hand of 'factitious historical inevitability' having been removed. But if it's only the composer's choice, why should it have any compelling force? Holloway's answer to that question is given later in his essay, where he says that 'the old obligations of choice, dexterity, control and organising of material, invention, taste, memory, conscious artistry are not lessened by that freedom'. But this simply pushes the same nagging question back a stage further. What determines the particular form that choice, dexterity, control, etc. take? These are things whose

manifestation in music is always historically determined; control and taste mean something very
different in Josquin and Schoenberg. But Holloway has banished history *ex hypothesi* so again
the answer is: the composer's choice. It could be
Ligeti micropolyphony one day, species counterpoint the next.

It's a strange idea, that the future direction of
art music should be entrusted to something so
frivolous. Holloway's idea reminds me of the fate
of music in Hesse's *The Glass Bead Game*, where
music has been 'rescued' from history by an army
of bloodless scholars, who patiently recompose
the music of the past. As a result it takes on a
strange pallid quality, very like the one displayed
by today's fusion musics. It is the connection with
history and with social forms that gives music life,
even so apparently an abstract art as classical
music. The modernists at least have the virtue of
seeing that the composer's predicament cannot be
solved by a historical sleight-of-hand, and that the
stance towards vocabulary and language must be
authentically of the present moment. The trouble
is that their solution to a historical problem is as
vehemently ahistorical as the one chosen by the
neo-tonal composers like Holloway. In trying to
escape from the deadening influence of consumerism, and what Lachenmann calls 'the tautological
use of pre-existing forms', they fly to the opposite
extreme. The music of Ferneyhough, or Dillon or

Richard Barrett refuses any engagement with historical forms and practices that is not heavily ironic, or 'deconstructed', to the point where they become unrecognizable. The result is a music that resists not just the sticky embrace of consumerism, but any form of collective, socially sanctioned meaning.

Alongside, or behind the problems of modern music specifically lies the more general question of whether the category of classical music still has value. It may be doubted whether our culture any longer needs the kind of 'depth' that classical music gives. Perhaps the locus of value has moved elsewhere. After all, there's no reason to think the model of musical and human value posited in classical music is eternal. It came into being at a certain historical moment, and that moment has perhaps now passed.

If that were true, then classical music would in a certain sense be becoming invisible. This sounds an implausible claim when, thanks to movie sound-tracks, commercials and chill-out compilation CDs, we're more surrounded by classical music than ever. But just because something is all round us doesn't mean we notice it, or understand its value – rather the reverse. The fact that electronica can now be referred to as symphonic, and that chill-out music can receive a classical CD award, is surely evidence that classical music is in fact becoming foreign and distant. It's no longer part of people's lived experience, but is more like a memory which the latest blockbuster sound-track stirs into life. More and more, classical music manifests itself as an evocation, a flavour of something at once classy and sumptuously expressive, rather than as something lived and engaged with.

It's an alarming idea, that classical music might be becoming invisible and ubiquitous at the same moment. It prompts the desperate, but not entirely unserious thought that the best thing for classical music would be to vanish for 50 years, so that it could then be lovingly rediscovered. Unfortunately the chances of that happening are zero; so we have a choice, either to keep faith with classical music, and reanimate it so that it stays a living art; or be faced always with its ghost, murmuring at us from restaurant loudspeakers and CD shops and TV screens.

There's another reason we should cherish classical music, and more particularly its living composers. The rival claimants for 'depth' in music simply don't stack up. Let's look at them one by one, beginning with occasional music. There are the faint remnants of 'occasional' and functional music still at large in our culture, but they're too scattered and infrequent to add up to anything substantial. You can't make a musical culture out of nursery rhymes and Mendelssohn's *Wedding March*. Of course there's popular music, which you could say has the best sort of 'depth', in that it forms and articulates a culture as it comes into being. It's always authentically of now. But no sooner has it come into being than it's seized by commercial interests, and becomes an orthodoxy to be rebelled against. Thus we have that continual pattern whereby a rebellious new form of music arises, which then becomes the new orthodoxy, which again breeds rebellion. The dynamic, and the rhetoric, is exactly that of art music, but what's missing is the element of syntax, the craft, that gives the dialectic something to work on. So all we're left with is authenticity, which as we've seen is really nothing more than an attitude, an attitude all too easily struck by the untalented.

Then there's the music of belonging: the music of minority cultures and all the various subcultures. These are less subject to commercial pressures than pop, and they are, as we've seen, very much in favour with the Cultural Ministries. But precisely because they assert themselves as signs of belonging, their range of reference and appeal is necessarily small (the *apparatchiks* of Cultural Ministries know this, in their heart of hearts, which is why the demand for 'accessibility' laid so forcibly on classical music is never laid on these forms of music).

Alongside these musics, whose social narrowness is part of their definition, lie other kinds of music which are equally narrow in their appeal.

But here the narrowness doesn't arise out of social function (as it does in, say, Sephardic music, which was a very narrow sort of music serving the needs of Sephardic Jews, until it was bought out by world music). A musical genre like 'sample-delia' becomes the choice of a very narrow range of listeners, whose only connection is the music itself. But a narrow social grouping defined by a value-system baffling to the world at large is a rough-and-ready definition of a cult. And this music does indeed have a cultish air, which in some strange way informs our experience of the sounds themselves (unless we're numbered among sampledelia's devotees, of course, in which case the music seems as natural as breathing). The same exclusive air clings to the discourse round these sorts of music, which multiplies jargon terms in a way that almost seems intended to keep the casual reader away. Few things are less 'accessible' than that Baedeker of left-field music, *The Wire*.

So, what we have is a range of musics all with an unimpeachable claim to depth; but it's not a depth than anyone outside the group can share, because its criteria are defined within the group. Meanwhile, as all these niche musics pursue their own aims, behind their backs another kind of music arises inexorably, which seems to be hospitable to them, but really wants to take them over.

It's the form of music whose 'classical' manifestations I discussed in the last chapter, but which doesn't really belong in classical music, or ambient music, or pop, or world music. Or rather, it belongs in all those places. I'll call it 'global music' to distinguish it from world music. It's the musical analogue of globalization, in that its technology and ethos is Western but the surface sound can be from East or West, high or low. It's that curious borderland between world and ambient music and lush film score where so much of the world's music seems to dwell. Like globalization, it follows a logic of unstoppable expansion, and, also like globalization, it destroys all the traditional meanings and memories and forms of life it finds in its path.

What kind of musical practice can resist something so powerful? Only one: Western classical music. It can resist it because its basis is rational and democratic, the one attribute implying the other. The things that make classical music a quintessentially Western phenomenon – its rules, its techniques, the distinction it draws between idea and realization, surface and depth – are indeed the things which makes it democratic. Anyone can join classical music's magic space, if they take a little trouble to learn its ways. And when they do join it, they'll find that those rules and techniques aren't fabricated *de novo*, on purely rational principles. They've arisen out of a real social practice, over the course of centuries. This is the true marvel of classical music: it is both traditional and rational, both inside history and out of it.

It is because classical music stands on three legs – rationality, democracy, tradition – that it's so immensely sturdy. But tradition was the one that had to go, in the eyes of many modernist composers. The 'realm of music' was too badly fissured and eroded to allow any half-measures; root and branch reform was needed. The result, as we've seen in previous chapters, is a music that was, and is, impressive in its fierce purity. But without tradition, standing on only two legs, modern classical music is a less sturdy beast; in fact it can seem no less cultish than some of the niche musics I've been describing.

There's no doubt that modernist classical music has had in the past a narrow base of listeners, an arcane jargon, and a certain tendency to solemnity. And this has badly compromised its claim to the kind of seriousness that 'old' classical music claims. But it's getting over that. Now that its vocabulary and techniques are passing into the wider musical world, modernism is losing its cultishness (it must be said this can be at the cost, in a composer like Macmillan, of a degree of sentimentality; but it doesn't have to be). Composers have discovered that integrity needn't entail fierce purity, or adherence to a system; treading the *via negativa* of the extreme modernists isn't the only way of saving music from being delivered, bound and gagged, into the servitude of 'evocation'. The recent music of composers as various as Ligeti, Judith Weir, John Zorn and Brett Dean shows that it is possible, after all, to connect a genuinely contemporary practice with classical music's past, without slipping into reach-me-down expressivity.

Linking contemporary art music to its past is one essential step to restoring it to full life. But a sceptic might ask – what about classical music's connection with the present, and potential for the future? Surely classical music needs to regain the thing that once made it so strong – a connection with the musical vernacular? The model always held out to us is Mozart's Vienna, where the melodies of Mozart's operas were no sooner heard in the opera house than they were transferred out to the street, to join the great river of 'folk music'. The great difference with our time was that there was indeed *one* vernacular for Mozart to join with, namely music of 'the folk'. But for us there is no *one* vernacular, there are numerous vernaculars, within different genres, and different subcultures. And there's no pressing necessity for a composer to choose one rather than another. Everything is equally available, 'from bhangra to bluegrass' as the phrase has it. It's interesting that the most successful examples of a classical practice fusing with a chosen 'vernacular' are the ones where choice does indeed seem necessary.

The stream of overtly Jewish-flavoured works produced by John Zorn in the 1990s surely get their urgency from the fact that, through creating these works, Zorn was reclaiming a Jewish identity. Without that urgent felt engagement, the incorporation of pop or world music sources can slip all too easily into a consumerist aesthetic of 'fusion', where the parade of flavours becomes the limit of the music's ambition. This isn't to say that the engagement between classical music and world music or pop is necessarily a bad thing; only that it is fraught with ironies, and doesn't by any means provide a straight and easy path to spontaneity and emotional truth.

Underlying the desire for classical music to 'fuse' with other musics is the thought that any art-form must be 'in tune with the times' to be truly alive. In music this means connecting, not just with 'the vernacular' – however one defines that – but with contemporary forms of technology. One criticism of many classical musicians is that they are 'stuck in the prison of purely acoustic performance'.[8] The implication is that the concepts and the principles of the musical realm – particularly things like the relationship between text and sound – are bound up with outmoded technologies, and that if only classical music could embrace new technology, a new idea of the musical realm would come into being.

It's one of those ideas that seems unanswerable in its simplicity. Actually it's not so simple. The experience of Paul Lansky, one of the most interesting and thoughtful of the composers who create their music largely with computers, shows that the old categories aren't so easy to shake off. Back in the 1980s, Lansky was convinced that the old linear relationship of composer-performer-listener was being replaced by an 'open network', in which two new roles would be equally important: the 'sound giver' and the 'instrument builder'. But now he's sceptical about the network idea; indeed he's sceptical about 'the hype that so often accompanies arguments about the freedom that technology brings to people who haven't undergone extensive musical training'.[9] The hint here that there is a musical realm which is prior to new technical means, to which the new means must be subservient, is born out later in the same interview, where Lansky says 'my perspective is that rather than trying to liberate our musical perceptions from traditional notions of music, I'm interesting in harnessing the world-building power of familiar musical conceptions to enhance our perceptions of the sounds of the world'.[10] But the really interesting part of the interview comes when Lansky explains the ways in which he tries to reconceive the relationship between creator and listener:

> It's really a problem, writing music that essentially lives on tape or CD, because you're bypassing the whole performance process. ... One strategy [to avoid the debilitating effects of that bypassing] is to build in a kind of distance so your relation with the music is oblique: it doesn't tell you right out what it is you're supposed to do with yourself as you listen to it. In the case of *Still Time*, I built an expansive and 'not-right-at-the-tip-of-your-nose' sort of continuity, which is modelled more on cinematic logic than on traditional notions of musical continuity.[11]

This has the pleased air of a man who thinks he's hit on something. In fact all Lansky's done is restate the age-old principle of classical music. We *always* have a distant, oblique relation with a piece of classical music, if it's good. And the idea of a discontinuous form of musical discourse, modelled on cinematic cross-cutting, has been a leading idea of modern music ever since Satie's 'Relâche', now nearly a century old.

Paul Lansky is actually more traditional than he realizes. And this is bound to be the case, because once you throw in your lot with art music, you have to accede to the idea that being contemporary, being of now, is all to do with actualizing the past in the present. The past is your vernacular. Once again we come back to the mysterious dual nature of classical music. It is both historical (its products come, by and large, from the past) and contemporary, in that its leading ideas, its conception of the 'musical realm', are still alive, and still the best guide we have to what musical value consists in.

That conception, at bottom, is that music only serves us well when we submit to it. Other musical practices share that intuition, but classical music actually gives that intuition some substance, in the form of a set of pieces and techniques, and an entire metaphysics of music, that one can share and pass on, even to people in cultures far distant to our own. So am I going to end with a plea to restore classical music's hegemony, which it seems to be on the point of losing? I'd be content with something apparently more modest, but perhaps no less impossible to achieve – an honesty in our critical language, an end to the ideology of 'breaking down barriers', and an admission that distinctions really do matter. What I am pleading for is a genuine plurality, not the fake one we have at present. The growth of fusion, and the kind of subjectivity it inculcates, is unstoppable – it needs no help from anyone, least of all arts centres and Arts Councils. What does need help is the sense that music has human possibilities beyond the purveying of fantasy. In this task of restoring distinctions classical music suddenly has a crucial role to play. As it loses its privileged status, its formal and human qualities can shine forth, unclouded by resentment.

The other essential step in keeping contemporary art music healthy is to change the musical culture from a passive to an active one. There are encouraging signs that this is already happening. It is in the moment that music is made that the past becomes actualized in the present, so rescuing the present from the fatal thinness it normally has in our amnesiac culture. There was a time when music always rose to that majestic destiny; and it could do so again, if only people's relationship to music were felt in their fingers and in their throats, rather than simply registered by their ears, in a distracted way, while busy with something else. And if people were to embrace singing and playing as part of their lives, they would really discover how to listen. And it is only when people discover how to listen that music can be freed from its subservience to words, and revived as a true resisting medium, whose 'grain' is made up, not of interesting sounds, but of musical entities. These musical entities are constituted by practices that are both rule-bound (they can be formally specified) and determined by social practices.

Both these aspects are equally vital. If there's one thing the history of modern music has taught us, it is that composers cannot reassemble the musical realm by themselves, from first principles. But an active music-making people can. Make the musical culture an active one, and the musical realm will eventually reconfigure itself, in ways we can't now imagine. The old dichotomies of 'cheap' and 'shallow', 'high' and 'low' would be redrawn, or perhaps even disappear. If that were to happen, then we could let classical music go without so much as a backward glance, because it would no longer be needed. Our music-making would give us a real lived connection between past and present, a connection for which classical music is, after all, only a beautiful metaphor.

It's a wonderful prospect, but of course it's Utopian, because it implies a common musical culture; whereas all the signs are that the future for Western democracies is of a diversity of musical cultures, each with their own practices. So, once again, we're brought back to the special mission of classical music. If we cannot have a real musical Utopia, with a single universal practice that unites present and past, let us at least preserve the imaginative possibility of such a marvellous thing. And that possibility is what classical music holds out to us. We need to be musically bilingual, in our own local musical culture and this stupendous 'musical realm' which anyone can enter.

Restoring a value and a weight to the present moment has a corollary which some people would find uncomfortable. Because there is, after all, something pleasant about our current 'amnesiac' state. Self-forgetfulness and distraction are forms of emotional anaesthesia they keep both pain and joy at bay. One source of pain that distraction keeps at arm's length is the awareness of our own mortality, an awareness with which music has a deep connection. It's made clear in Leonardo's meditation on music's nature:

> Music may be called the sister of painting, for she is dependent on hearing, the sense which comes second, and her harmony is composed of the union of its proportional parts sounded simultaneously, rising and falling in one or more harmonic rhythms. ... But painting excels and ranks far higher than music, because it does not fade away as soon as it is born, which is the fate of unhappy music ...[13]

But nowadays music does not fade away as soon as it is born. Music is always with us; the roar of music across the airwaves and across the internet never ceases, until we choose to turn our back on it. The essential fact about music, which is that it dies, and has to die in order for it to glorify *this* present moment happening *now*, is systematically denied in our passive musical culture, just as mortality is denied. The result is precisely the lack of emotional intensity that Jung observed in contemporary life, and which we can observe in those forms of music most symptomatic of the present day. Restoring that intensity is something we crave, but we never think that its lack may be partly in ourselves, and with the way we relate to music. Instead we instinctively delegate. In pop music and world music, we look always for performers with that mysterious *daemon*, and in art music we look for composers with some special 'vision' that will seize us like a revelation. But perhaps we've delegated for too long. Perhaps it's time to look to ourselves.

NOTES

1. Kolb, B. (2000). 'The Effect of Generational Change on Classical Music Concert Attendance and Orchestras', *Cultural Trends*, 41. London, Policy Studies Institute.

2. Walden, G. (2001). *The New Elites: Making a Career in the Masses*. London, Allen Lane.

3. See for example Johann Adolf Scheibe's *Critischer Musicus* (1745). Scheibe suggests that instrumental music, because it cannot speak or represent anything, is 'mere noise'.

4. Eagleton, T. (1990). *The Ideology of the Aesthetic*. Oxford, OUP, quoted in Miller, S. (ed.) (1993). *The Last Post: Music after Modernism*. Manchester, Manchester University Press, pp. 16–17.

5. Holloway, R. (2001). 'Modernism and After', in Davison, P. (ed.). *Reviving the Muse: Essays on Music after Modernism*. Brinkworth, UK, Claridge Press, pp. 93–111.

6. *Ibid.*, p. 109.

7. *Ibid.*, p. 105.

8. Richard Wolfson, *Daily Telegraph*, London, 6 January 2001.

9. From http://silvertone.princeton.edu/~paul/perry.interview.html

10. *Ibid.*

11. *Ibid.*

12. Richter, Irma A. (ed.) (1977). *Selections from the Notebooks of Leonardo da Vinci*. Oxford, Clarendon Press, quoted in Bujic, B. (1993). 'Notation and Realisation', in Krausz, M. (ed.). *The Interpretation of Music: Philosophical Essays*. Oxford, Clarendon Press, p. 136.

Index

INDEX

INDEX